HIDING BEHIND THE LIPSTICK

MYESHA CHANEY

Hiding Behind the Lipstick
Copyright © 2014 by Myesha Chaney

Scripture quotations, unless otherwise noted are taken from THE HOLY BIBLE, NEW INTERNATIONAL VERSION®, NIV® Copyright © 1973, 1978, 1984, 2011 by Biblica, Inc.® Used by permission. All rights reserved worldwide.

ISBN 978-0-9894934-6-8
eISBN 978-0-9894934-8-2

Fedd Books
Post Office Box 341973
Austin, TX 78734
www.thefeddagency.com

Published in association with the literary agency of
The Fedd Agency, Inc.

Editorial services by Layce Smith
Cover photo by Phœnix White
Cover design by Chris Valcarcel

Printed in the United States of America
First Edition 2014

I dedicate this book to my Lord and Savior, Jesus Christ, thank you for trusting me. To my husband and best friend, Wayne A. Chaney, Jr., I love you. My children, Wayne Chaney III, Reign Chaney, and Cadence Chaney, you are all my heart. My entire family, loved ones, and church family, thank you for your undying love and support. For those that have been on this mission with me, I appreciate you so much.

Table of Contents

PREFACE

I was in prison—a prison only felt in an intangible realm—my insecurities were the bars that held me, disappointment was my cellmate, and fear was my guard. Locked down by emotions, thought patterns, and ideals that did not match my reality, I was stuck in the futility of my own mind and captive to my own thoughts. The result was a false identity. The person I presented to the world wasn't really me.

Every day I put on a mask. No one knew the truth. No one knew my prison. On the outside it seemed I had it all together when, in fact, I was hiding behind the lipstick. I felt as if I were in bondage, chained to the person everyone expected me to be. I was a fully-functioning, enslaved woman trying to live life. Darkness was never this black.

During this time, I found refuge in the pool of hopes and dreams that never dried up. Mustering all of the courage and strength within me, I went on a mission—a secret mission—to prove wrong those who sat on the jury that convicted me of such an innocent crime. I was charged with just trying to be me. I was driven by things that did not reflect my true self, gifts, or abilities, but by things everyone said I should do. An increasing amount of passion began to exude from me. It radiated around me and consumed me.

I gave in. I officially had a stain on my record, guilty as charged. I didn't know who I was. I was like a boxer with flailing arms, striking the air, swinging with all his might, only to have his opponent deliver a blow that would knock him out. That was my story. I was swinging blindly at so many areas, trying to prove things to so many people, and trying to be accepted in so many ways that I was losing the fight to preserve me.

As I spent the next few years refining the fictitious person within me, I discovered a newfound toughness. I adopted necessary methods to accomplish the "task at hand." In my haste to complete goals, I didn't stop for one second to do a reality check to see if everything I said I was matched who I really was deep down inside. What a tragedy it is to gain so much (survival skills) yet to lose the scent of perfection the Potter breathed when He finished His creation: me.

The weight of frustration began to worry me, so I tried to break out. I was upset with the condition I found myself in. I started to blame others for not helping me. Found only in the inner chambers of my heart were the questions: *Why didn't they warn me? Why didn't anyone protect me? How did I get in this situation? Who am I? Where am I? What is God's plan for me?*

I was running myself dry trying to fit other people's expectations of me, and I wanted it to stop. I wanted to discover who I really was deep down inside. What did I enjoy? What was my fashion sense? What were my personal convictions? These were the questions I asked myself. I didn't like who I was becoming, and I couldn't continue to live as someone else for much longer. I wanted out of the falsehood. I wanted to return to infancy and depend on the loving, gentle care of another. I wanted to start all over, hide under a rock for about twelve months until I got my head on straight. I was supposed to be happy, but a piece of me felt like I was severely oxygen deprived. When someone asked me how I was doing, I wanted to respond by saying, "life sucks." I was tired, tired of being sad yet pretending I was overjoyed. I was tired of looking good on the outside while feeling terrible on the inside. I was tired of playing the game others played, tired of competing, of retreating, and covering things up; I was tired of hiding.

After spending dedicated time in prayer, I decided it was time to make some bold discoveries about what my freedom would require. I had to confront everything about my existence and challenge those beliefs about myself that were somehow picked up along life's journey. Suddenly my metaphoric eyes were opened and I saw myself from a different vantage point: God's. Our humanity is frail and flawed yet so perfectly cared for by God.

I wanted to help others experience the freedom I began to feel and to share a new way of viewing life. My newfound revelation sparked a much-needed sensitivity to others. I began to truly see the condition of the women in my church, and my heart was persuaded to deep conviction. I was enchained and they were too. We were all hiding. Our conversations were superficial and trust was not fully present. We all had our guards up. We pretended to have true love for one another when we were simply just waiting to be loved. There we were, a bunch of unwitting slaves, searching for answers to the faint questions disturbing our spirits. Just a cluster of women experiencing great things devoid of true expression—we were without meaningful, enriching relationships. And it was time for that to change.

Then the opportunity came. It was our annual women's retreat. Quiet whispers filled the meeting room. Women from all geographic regions gathered together to sip from the fountain, the life source. They came to hear from Him—to be rejuvenated. They sat in eager anticipation for what would take place this night. And in the middle of this congregation's deep yearning and questioning presence, there I was.

The journey to the ballroom was quiet. There was no enthusiastic pep talk; it was only a bland exchange of random thoughts drifting through my mind. There was a back and forth tug, a North and South notion, a distraction; it was wrestling for my will. Fear had come to silence my voice. But I resisted and it fled. It was time. It had to be done. I had to do it.

Although frightened, I moved. Through my nervousness, I stepped out. Even in my insecurity, I found confidence. While shaking, I stood. And, in the face of doubt, I trusted. How could I tell them that the very foundation on which we all lived was wrong? How could I remove the mask? How could I speak about these issues publicly? Although challenging, I did it. I spoke candidly to all who would listen about the areas of our lives in which we falter. We so often pride ourselves on having the perfect marriage, a successful career, or money in our bank account when in reality we are miserable in marriage, ready for a change in our career, and living paycheck to paycheck. It was time for accountability in what we project to the public and to bring forth the truth of who we are.

I went out as David before Goliath, with slingshot and stones, ready to take out the giant that had been torturing us all. It was time to snatch the keys from the prison guard, unlock all the jail cells, and free the prisoners. A movement needed to begin for the sake of this generation and those to come. This recurring cycle of us creating our perfect reality, hiding the truth, trying to fix our failures, living a lie, and feeling empty on the inside needed to be broken.

Who would have thought that out of the obedience of one, hundreds would be free? The message of "Hiding Behind the Lipstick" gently took us through a process of self-discovery. It gave us the boldness to stand before a room full of people and share our truth. One woman after another confessed what she was hiding behind. We witnessed first-hand vulnerability and openness that led to the creation of an unbreakable bond of sisterhood. For the first time, we actually knew each other. "Hiding Behind the Lipstick" was an experience that transformed us from the inside out. We were liberated, not to mention in touch with the beauty of our true selves.

The sun never had shone as brightly as it did on this day. Nor had the flowers ever produced a fragrance that could be bottled and sold for millions of dollars like they had on this day. This day was like a rare eclipse that could only be seen once in a lifetime from mars, and we saw it! Witnessing the freedom of so many lives was refreshing and beautiful. Our exchange of heartfelt sentiments was peaceful yet powerful. It was hearts meeting hearts and true compassion uniting us together.

The rest of the night, we nestled comfortably in any fragment of space and listened to story after story, testimony after testimony of what Hiding Behind the Lipstick meant to each brave soul. Women shared what taking the mask off signified for them. We cried, laughed, hugged, encouraged each other, prayed, and developed a special bond in our most vulnerable moments. It was the first time that pure honesty had poured out among this group of women. Everyone shared things about themselves that no one else knew—things they were hiding behind, embarrassed about, ashamed of, afraid of, and that made them smile. It was one of the most amazing experiences of my life. And it is what inspired the penning of this book. It was the motivation to share with scores more that hiding can be a thing of the past and that openness is nothing to fear. Much of what was spoken to that group of women on that day was placed in this book and is now available to you.

Real freedom and truth cannot be bought, borrowed, or copied. Those who earnestly desire it will seek it and will find it. Real freedom is being able to take the mask off and show the mixed-up, jacked-up, hurt, insecure, not-having-it-all-together self that we have suppressed all along. Freedom is having the ability to tap into the wealth of resources within ourselves for the sake of helping others. It is allowing all of our unique experiences to become a catalyst of change for someone else.

How can one ever see the light of day after losing precious moments in the prison of the mind? It is possible. Like the ringing of a clock, signaling the start of a new week, we are sounding the alarm and awakening ourselves to a new day with new challenges and new opportunity. May the gleam of hope and light at the end of the tunnel be visible to you with the conclusion of this book. I pray that you are enlightened, inspired, and willing to come out of hiding. Embrace the attributes, feelings, gifts, purposes, and goals that mean most to you. Share with others who you really are. Stop hiding behind the lipstick.

INTRODUCTION

Hiding Behind the Lipstick is a summation of ideas that provoke women to realistically and practically become who they are meant to be. It dismantles the lies. It destroys the counterfeit and the façades that we present to those we come in contact with. It helps women become honest with themselves about what they feel, what they think, and where they are going. The ultimate goal of *Hiding Behind the Lipstick*® is to free women from self-constructed prisons and encourage them to express all the gifts, talents, and abilities that were trapped in the process.

Through the restoration of genuine contentment in life, this book will work to preserve the integrity of a generation. Each day we should consciously perform a self-assessment. *Hiding Behind the Lipstick* will trigger an inner reflection of one's primary desires, passions, and deeply-rooted connection to their essence. It will bring us to a humbling place and cause us to experience vulnerable love and true compassion toward one another.

We desperately need to return to the foundational principles of giving and receiving love, having the discipline to deal with painful situations (both past and future), staying in tune with our feelings, having an honest sense of ourselves, and living in our purpose. These will cause us to flourish and prosper. We need to have the freedom to express the good, the bad, the ugly, the hardship, the frustration, the hurt, the pressure to produce, the disappointment, the disgust, the lack of inspiration, the diminished motivation, and the current condition of our being.

Our quality of life rests in our ability to emerge as our true self. Countless hours go into fixing mistakes, playing a role, hiding the truth, and pretending to be happy. By spending our precious time playing a role not reflective of our true self, we miss out on the emotional rest and subsequent contentment that comes from being the person we really are. *Hiding Behind the Lipstick* is a one-way ticket to experiencing freedom in ways you never thought possible.

Are you ready? Well, like any exciting road trip, there is preparation involved. No one decides to drive cross-country without checking the tires, making sure the spare is in place, and getting an oil change. You now have an opportunity to prepare your heart for the miles that lie ahead. This adventure toward self-discovery is truly the first step at gaining strength that has been lost and the confidence and self-love you desperately need.

You currently stand braced between two realities. You can continue driving the car you have known your entire life—custom-equipped with all of your mistakes, fully-loaded with past experiences and newly-installed internal struggles, polished on the outside, but showing the years of wear and tear life has imprinted in the upholstery; or you can decide to leave that car, memories and all, sitting on the side of the road and walk with a new lease on life.

Make the choice to proceed with an open heart, an open mind, and a willing spirit to allow true transformation to take its course. Lose yourself. Release yourself for a brief moment. Be vulnerable. Examine who you are. There is no injustice in deciding that you are not ready to take the ride. Just know there are lives connected to you, waiting for you, so that they too may be free. Your family, friends, and co-workers are desperate for change. The kind of change they may only see in you. Your decision to start this journey may improve the quality of life for the women you know and love.

In order to get the most out of this book, you must determine in your heart that you will open yourself up to the truth. This is about a process that will ultimately bring freedom in different areas of your life. I mean free for real this time. Commit to private and intimate moments with yourself. Be willing to try something new and different for a change. Leave behind all your stereotypes and hang-ups. Begin to release the control you have over your life and your emotions. This will be a journey that you will never forget.

There is a place, a depth, within ourselves that we are heading toward. Our families, friends, and generations to come are dependent upon the decisions we make to-day. Our actions and attitudes directly or indirectly affect those whom we may never come in contact with.

I never had the opportunity to meet my father's mother. But her willingness to provide for her family, feed and care for the kids in the neighborhood, and constantly spend time in prayer has shown through the attributes of my father. He has a heart for the community because of what he saw his mother do as he was growing up. We should see our life as a spark that could light a fire in the generations to come.

Owning the fact that the choices we make in our

lives can affect our offspring is the beginning of adopting a "transgenerational" view. Our daughters pay attention to how we live at home and how we perform in public. The mother who publicly prides herself on having the perfect American family, yet is repeatedly physically abused, putting makeup over her black eyes, has a daughter mentally taking notes and making decisions about how she will deal with similar issues in her future.

Our decisions can affect those around us whether positively or negatively. Change will start with you. After reading this book and deciding to embrace all facets of who you are, your children's children will be exposed to the best you that you can be. In turn, they will have a better chance to be the best them that they can be.

As you know, whenever you intend to do what is good, evil is always present. It is a fight to pry away a faulty self-image. It is a battle to silence the voices that have murmured so long. It is a challenge to convince those who don't have your best intentions at heart that this is really who you are. It is hard to wipe away years of makeup. It might not be an easy feat, but trust that the victory was yours after reading the first page of this book. Get a glimpse of yourself at the finish line, because you have already won.

PRIMER

Just as we use primer on our faces before applying makeup, God primes (or prepares) us for the work He has for us to do. This process is unique to each person. We all face different situations in life. Both the joys and hardships we experience shape our "true selves" for the purpose of bringing us closer to each other as we move closer to God. If we are going to stop hiding behind the lipstick, we need to go back to the most basic tool in our makeup bag; we need to check our primer.

Primed for Relationship

Our lives are driven by the relationships we engage in or try to disassociate ourselves from. When we are primed for relationship, our hearts are prepared to invest in fundamental connections that will foster growth and ultimately shape our character. Whether some of these connections lead to positive or negative experiences, the fact always remains that we are relational beings.

Mary considers herself a loner. In her estimation, friendships and relationships are optional and hold little value. Her daily routine is simple: work, home, eat, sleep, and back to work. She says she doesn't have time for the emotional baggage that may come from letting people into her very private life.

Mary is hiding behind the lipstick of loneliness and self-preservation. The truth is that in her early twenties she fell head over heels in love with a man. He was her soul mate; but after two years of a wonderful relationship, her beloved decided he wanted to move on. Without much explanation, he left town and never looked back. Mary was absolutely devastated. She vowed that the pieces of her broken heart would never be put back together again. Her commitment to herself continues to keep everyone at a distance. While her natural tendency as a relational being is hidden, it is not lost. Buried under years of hard, painful seclusion, a vulnerable Mary is screaming to get out—to fulfill her purpose of loving and engaging with other people.

Each and every one of us has a deep sense of purpose. Contained within our being is the desire to be used for the betterment of others. We were created to connect, to engage in meaningful relationships, and to have compassion for people. If we eliminated the long mental register of hurts, disappointments, and pain, we would agree that fulfillment comes from genuinely offering aid to others. There needs to be a paradigm shift in our thought process. We need to see our lives as a springboard for someone else's freedom. We are all interconnected. It is impossible to begin to think of others if we are completely absorbed in ourselves. Just as cosmetic primer sets our makeup to last all day, our spiritual primer sets our hearts in tune with those around us for the purpose of building lasting relationships.

Primed for Depth

God wants to take us deeper. There is a place in our hearts that longs for an intimate relationship with Him. It doesn't matter how young or old you are. It doesn't even matter what you have done or where you have been. He desires to use you to fulfill His plans on the earth. He is drawing us closer and is bringing us to a place of maturity in His spirit. If we are to go deeper in worship and in our relationship with Him, we have to stop lying to ourselves about who we are and where we are.

God created us. He is comfortable with our emotional, physical, and spiritual composition, but our issues prevent us from embracing the truth of that. In order to be the people we are meant to be, our minds need to be willing to accept what our hearts already know: we are made to go deeper.

Since childhood, friendship was something I always longed for—not the casual kind of relationship filled with shopping and meaningless chatter, but the "jump in front of a train for my friend" kind. As I got older, I started to tell myself I wasn't supposed to have the type of friendships I craved. I created scenarios and thought patterns that justified why I didn't have the depth in my relationships I so desperately longed for.

After a husband and a few kids, I stopped lying to myself. It was clear I needed and wanted friendships; I just didn't have them. I enjoy being around others, but the realities of my life caused my view to be skewed. I adopted principles and beliefs that were not consistent with my earnest desires.

Primed for Boldness

Being bold about our characteristics, ideals, convictions, and current situations in life is embracing who we are. Ultimately, these things do not define us, but they do make us useful and impactful in our families, communities, and the world.

If we are unhappy, we shouldn't try to fake happiness. Doing so might mean we never get the help we need in order to experience true joy. If we are concerned about the public education system, we should take action instead of simply grumbling about it. Perhaps other women are just waiting for a leader to step up and call for change. If we are struggling financially, we should not fight to maintain our lifestyle of plenty. Even if it's hard to tell our children they can't have the newest and best items this month, setting the example of responsibility and self-discipline is more important than making sure their peers approve of them. We must embrace the facets of our lives we may not be proud of or excited about. This doesn't mean we have to live in unhappiness or remain stuck in a financial hole. My point is that honesty is an absolute necessity and it requires boldness. We have to be honest with ourselves, with God, and with others.

Perhaps you were never allowed to be real and honest about yourself. Maybe you grew up in a home where emotions were irrelevant. Maybe your controlling mother set high expectations for you and you've always felt pressured to perform. Every time you tried to convey your desires, you were shut down under the guise of doing whatever it took to make your family proud. You learned that what you really feel is not important enough, so you suppressed it. When all that matters is saving face, openness almost becomes a curse word.

When was the last time you admitted that you felt broken? Can you recall a time when you were deeply hurt and embraced it? Let me offer this disclaimer: you do not have to tell all of your personal business in order to be "real." I am not saying to go up to a random person and tell them your house is in foreclosure and you're losing everything you have. You don't have to share all of your insecurities or regrets. This is not some super religious confessional that requires you divulge your life story. You simply need to get to a place where you can admit you're having a bad day or feel scared or can't afford something.

When we project something other than our personal truth, we run the risk of losing an opportunity to uplift or encourage a person who needed the comfort of a common experience. God needs some authentic people who are willing to boldly yield to themselves for a greater good.

Primed to be Genuine

Have you ever knowingly bought fake Gucci™, Coach™, or Louis Vuitton™? (I am not judging you.) Now, what if you went to the Louis Vuitton™ store to purchase a genuine purse and realized it was an imitation when you got home? We could safely assume that you would be irate. You don't mind having something fake when it was your intention. You desired to have a replica and bought it. But there is a problem when you thought you were getting something authentic, and ended up with an imitation.

The definition of fake[1] is: one that is not what it purports itself to be; or a worthless imitation passed off as genuine. God wants real people who are honest and loving. He needs those who will help others navigate various circumstances in life. What use is it in joining people together who are lying about who they really are? Such interactions more aptly depict the world rather than His church.

People who are hurting want to come to God and experience something better than what the world has to offer. Being real about your flaws enables you to connect with others who may be experiencing similar difficulties in life. You become a tool to help those with whom you cross paths.

We all have scars of poor choices—the regret of missed moments, and wounds from just living life—but if we cover them with Band-Aids and pretend they never happened, we lose the opportunity to share our stories. We are primed for genuineness with one another.

No one is perfect, though society is constantly showing us what "perfection" looks like. The sad thing about this is that society views what's popular at a particular moment in time as perfection. We all have flaws both in our appearance and in our character. What we consider ideal today might be less than tomorrow.

> "If I shop where she shops, walk like she walks, and buy what she wears, then maybe I could be perfect too."

Contrary to our world's view, perfection is not fleeting; it is constant. Hiding the parts of ourselves that we feel don't measure up to societal expectations forces us to live an imperfect lie.

Whenever we find ourselves getting close to accepting our flaws, we see things on television, on social media, and in women around us that contradict the beautiful notion of being ourselves. We actually believe that if we shop where she shops, walks like she walks, and buy what she wears, then maybe we could be "perfect" too. It's a foolish notion that so many of us fall prey to.

Perfection will never be achieved by anyone on Earth. The moment you think you are close to it, life will happen, trends will change, or age will catch up with you. Being you at every stage of life is as close to perfection as you can possibly get. For this reason, it is vital that you embrace yourself for the sake of being genuine. Stop trying to imitate that woman who seems to have everything you desire. Stop tricking people into thinking you are something you're not. Trust that you will be accepted if you will just be genuine.

God has prepared our hearts in individual ways to deal with situations differently. He has given us different tastes and preferences to attract other people of different tastes and preferences. If we hide our genuine natures, then the chance for genuine relationships may be hidden from us as well.

Primed to Encourage

Do you ever wake up on the wrong side of the bed? You know, those days when things aren't going right. Maybe you awoke to bad news. After getting dressed, you noticed a hole in your only clean skirt. You got in your car to find the gas tank below empty. You stopped by the ATM and discovered your checking account was overdrawn. You finally make it to work only to find your parking spot has been taken, so you hike from the very end of the lot to the office in your most uncomfortable (however fabulous) heels.

Imagine, you finally make it to your desk—hair in a frizzy mess, mascara smudged, and feet on fire—and your co-worker leans over and tells you how smart and beautiful and important she thinks you are. It happened to be a very rough morning for you, and those comforting words were exactly what you needed to hear. Someone spoke life to you without knowing what was going on. Now, imagine you were that person to someone else. How amazing it is to be open and ready to speak as God leads with the sole purpose of encouraging others. Our goal should be to achieve wholeness as a person and to be confident enough in Him to do as He leads.

It is powerful to reserve the right to speak when necessary. We are naturally curious creatures; we don't need anyone's help to take notice of the people around us. The only step that might require some effort outside of our nature would be to actually say something. To be able to do so, if God leads, is a skill we must develop.

Everything that can be said may be permissible but may not always be beneficial in an individual's circumstance. We must be sensitive when discerning what is best to say and when. Ideally you should be in a place emotionally and spiritually that if you needed to help someone, you could do so without hesitation. Luckily, God has primed us to be encouraging people whether we are outgoing or not. Encouragement can take any form: it can manifest itself through words or actions.

We have to present our true nature in order for us to go deeper in God and understand how we have been primed for encouragement. If we are constantly showing a mere piece of the picture, telling part of the story, and compartmentalizing our experience with God, then we pre-suppose that He is only good for blessings and worship.

Change the mindset that *God is not telling me to say anything at the grocery store and is definitely not telling me to say anything to this girl I don't know.* God *is* saying, "take me out of that box; allow me to flow freely through you." Lose control for a second and allow Him to overtake you in a way that will totally transform your life. Be encouraged by his presence in your life and you will know how to be an encouragement for others.

Primed for His Plan

Primer keeps our makeup in place by allowing it to go on smoothly and blend well. During the day, as we are exposed to cold, heat, wind, humidity, and other elements, our makeup will appear fresh. When God primes us for His plan, He ensures that our experiences smooth our hurts, insecurities, and hesitations and provide a base for blending well with others in relationships.

When we allow Him, God makes sure that His plan for our life stays in place (even as we are tossed in the wind from time to time). Part of this requires us to see our need for primer. If we put our face on without primer and head out to go dancing for the night, we will most likely return home looking more disheveled than when we left.

Our own actions will cause this, but a proper base might have prevented our eye shadow from smudging or our blush from rubbing off on our sleeve.

Often, when we are presented with information that challenges our way of life, we receive it as though it pertains to someone else. We simply tell ourselves that our friend should read this or hear this without first seeing ourselves as the one in need. I want to offer you this suggestion: allow the need for primer to resonate with you personally. Let's look in the mirror and examine our own actions. It seems easier for us to determine areas of weakness for someone else and assess what they could do better, but we actually need to put ourselves first in this.

We are so filled with junk—lies, hurt, pain, frustration, questions, lust, wrestling, insecurity, layers of hardness, and disappointment—that it is very difficult for anything of truth and substance to penetrate our being. Some of us are so hard that a flicker of hope cannot even break through, making it more difficult for life change.

Maybe you have heard it all, seen it all, and determined in your heart that you just don't want to be primed for anything. This moment is a mere seed sown into your spirit that will influence your judgment the next time you are with people. You will be more conscious of the masks you wear, and my prayer is that when you deal with others you will see your actions from a different vantage point.

God has sent me on assignment to bring awareness of where we are, to spark thought, to begin the healing process, and to allow the Holy Spirit to dig deep within us. You are hiding behind the lipstick, but God has a plan for your life. When we become what our mothers trained us to be, what we think others will like, or what is the safest emotionally for us, we take His plan into our own hands. This is a process for women who are serious about their lives, their relationship with God, and the impact they will make on this world. We long for honesty and vulnerability, yet we often avoid exercising these traits ourselves. Take off the mask, show who you are, and allow others to love you, the real you, the person that God created you to be. And yes, all the flaws, mistakes, doubts, fears, passions, convictions, and accomplishments that come with the true you are absolutely welcome. If we can all do this, we will be an encouragement to one another by simply being our true selves. That is the purpose of God's primer.

My Lipstick Confession: I have always wanted a group of girlfriends. You know, like the cluster of college friends you see depicted in the movies. As I matured, I realized I really desired acceptance. Friendship provided a sense of belonging that I sought earnestly. My desires didn't prompt me to action though; instead I retreated. I hid behind my fear of rejection. I decided that friendships weren't for everyone and wholeheartedly committed myself to other "things." Because I was afraid I wouldn't fit in and wasn't good enough or worthy, I didn't want to fully open my heart to others. I most likely missed out on the establishment of very positive and nurturing female relationships because I bought into the lie that I was not primed for relationship.

Time to Reflect

Then you will know the truth, and the truth will set you free.

—John 8:32

Write one HONEST statement about yourself.
(Example: I was demoted today. It hurt my feelings.)

_____

_____

_____

_____

_____

Dear Lord,

Help me to be honest with myself. I don't want to live in deception any longer. I believe lies because I don't want to hurt. I want to look in the mirror and be in touch with the person you created me to be. I know you love me the way I am. Thank you.

Amen

HEAVY FOUNDATION

As I stated in the previous chapter, we have been primed for genuine relationships. However, rather than letting God apply the foundation of our being, we rely on others, and ourselves. The effect is a face that looks more universal with highlighted cheekbones, brow bones, and nose bridges and deeply contoured jaw lines, chins, and temples. When it's all said and done, our heavily applied foundation makes us look like the more generic idea of beauty and less like the unique creation God had in mind when we were being primed.

God gives us a foundation built on the creation He made us to be. By presenting that person to the world, we stay even and balanced. There is no reason to lie or cover up the truth because the truth is all that we have put forth. If the truth is not enough for us, then we pile on layer after layer of heavy foundation and hope the world only notices what aspects of ourselves we have tried to draw attention to.

Great Pretenders
You are hiding, hiding, hiding. Even if I wanted to I could not find you. Maybe you can't even find yourself. You are

present, holding this book, but you are officially withdrawn from life and have left the building. Your body is living, and you bustle about in the redundancy of your daily responsibilities, but you have lost the fervor and passion for your own existence. The lights are on but nobody is home.

Who are you? Who are you, really? What goes on in that head of yours? What happened to you? When we become so much to so many people, we lose our true identities. We just don't know who *we* are, what *we* like, what pleases *us,* or what is best for *our* own lives. We allow the desires and the happiness of other people to mislead and shipwreck the internal peace and security of our own identity. An overwhelming desire for love and relationships causes us to try to become all things to all men. It happens to best of us.

Maybe you meet an attractive man who just so happens to be six-foot-five, well dressed, well spoken, not to mention rich, and clearly out of your league. In his haste to get his Mercedes-Benz from the valet, he mentions he is going rock climbing on Saturday. In an attempt to garner his approval (and an invitation) you ramble off a lie about how much you love rock climbing and agree to go buy some new gear with him. Honestly, your last rock climb was at an amusement park when you were twelve, and you hated it. Nevertheless, you are willing to take up the dreaded hobby and spend hundreds of dollars on equipment if it gets you a date.

A part of us would rather learn to be comfortable with things we despise, in order to gain what we think we want, rather than stay true to who we are and receive the kind of love we actually deserve. It's the same as putting on tons of foundation to change the look of our faces rather than using a thin layer to stay even and balanced. Being who you are and loving it is the best gift you could ever give yourself. But that's hard to do with the wrong motivation, and especially the wrong foundation.

When we allow others to influence our thoughts and actions—when we use too much of the wrong foundation, we lose more and more of ourselves. God has tasks for us that may or may not involve the good-looking rock climber but that will certainly allow us to participate in his plan of redemption. In our masks of false identity and with our misplaced expectations, we unintentionally hide ourselves from Him as we pretend to have features that don't quite suit us.

In the Moment

> She did not consider her future. Her fall was astounding; there was none to comfort her.
> —Lamentations 1:9

God wants to use you to accomplish His purposes on Earth. When the assignment comes up on heaven's job board, God considers you for the task. He can't use you, however, if you are not the person He prepared you to be.

Maybe you are taking life into your own hands by making choices that gratify your current condition without considering your future, and then wondering why it feels like your prayers are not being answered. Have you considered that God had a specific purpose in mind when He created you? When you shape yourself into what you think will make you popular, desirable, or successful, you have put on too much foundation and are neglecting your intended purpose.

A motor vehicle is created to drive. We can decide to make it a home, a bed, a closet, or whatever else suits our fancy, but its optimal performance will be seen when it is carrying passengers down the street. You are at an optimal level suitable for mutual love, success, peace, and financial security when you operate according to your owner's manual. You can't even read the manual when you are buried under a heavy foundation applied by the pressures of others.

At times, God works on our hearts and leads us to do something different—something that is outside of the character we have always portrayed, so we choose not to do it. He might lead you to stop and talk to a homeless man, but your first thought is concern for your safety. The truth is you probably have put yourself in more dangerous situations before at parties and nightclubs. If God asks you later to go talk to a woman sitting alone at a coffee shop, what's your excuse then? Maybe she's crying and you don't want to upset her further. Maybe you don't want to make her feel uncomfortable. Maybe you just don't want anyone to see you comforting a perfect stranger (after all, they might think you're weird).

Living in the moment leads to choices that affect the future. If you choose to ignore God's call now, it will be easier to ignore Him the next time. Just because you have declared yourself (or been deemed by others) a certain "type" doesn't mean that is who you are and must always be. That is the weight of having the wrong foundation. When it's based on what or who people say you are, there is no freedom to become the person God is calling you to be.

Turning Inward

She did it. She graduated Magna Cum Laude from the most prestigious university in the state. Monica was on cloud nine. As a first generation graduate, her family was so proud of her.

A couple of years after graduation, Monica's friends moved into their respective vocations, got married, and started families. When they'd reconnect at weddings and other events, Moni-

> "I have 2 degrees and a PhD but I'd give it all up to have somebody love me."

ca would always have to put up with them trying to set her up with someone. To deal with the embarrassment they made her feel about being alone, she frequently boasted that she was finishing her doctorate degree while they were at home changing diapers.

After each wedding, Monica had to face her reality as she drove home alone, crying her eyes out. Being single wasn't her desire. She hid behind her accomplishments because she longed for a relationship. She didn't have the courage to be honest with anyone about her feelings. She accomplished more hoping that it would satisfy her longing for love and acceptance.

One night while sitting at the dinner table, waiting for

her food to warm, Monica solemnly wrote on a napkin: *I have two degrees and a Ph.D., but I'd give it all up to have somebody love me.*

Turning from concerning ourselves with the expectations of others enables us to better appreciate who we are. However, we must be careful not to take this to the extreme. Sometimes, rather than turning to God for the truth of ourselves, we put up walls around us that say "Keep Out." Like Monica, rather than loving ourselves in order to experience healthy relationships, we might end up rejecting relationships instead. When our foundation is one of pride or vanity, we are still missing the mark, and we still are not putting forth the person we were made to be.

There will come a time when you will want someone to be there for you. As life continues, you will experience things that knock the breath out of you. There may come a time when your marriage begins to fail. How comforting would it be to have someone who has a reconciled marriage to be a listening ear or someone who has experienced divorce to offer some encouragement?

Pain has the ability to alter our perspective. It changes the lens by which we view issues in life. If we hide behind our wall of ego, then we alienate ourselves from others who might be able to comfort us in times of need.

A person who is willing to share their story definitely helps us understand in the moment. The evidence of God's work in another person's life can be a source of hope in trying times. It's not just a matter of what other people can do for you, either. Think about the people you can help if you are willing to be open about your insecurity, pain, and lessons learned.

If I act as if my marriage is perfect, how will the person with the failing marriage know where to turn? If I am unable to be open and honest about things in life, whether good or bad, then someone struggling spiritually and/or emotionally may go without the help they need. We assume the more open we are the more ammunition others will have to use against us. We would rather be lone rangers and keep to ourselves to prevent any sort of drama. There is so much more we stand to gain by being open. It is liberating and freeing. Instead, we make excuses to keep ourselves behind the mask. We convince ourselves that this is the best way to live because the unknown territory of exposure is too frightening to comprehend. We can find being angry to be an acceptable way of life until we encounter how real joy feels.

A Step Back

At times we get caught in the hustle and bustle of life. We are so driven in our daily tasks and responsibilities that we forget to ask ourselves the question, *How am I doing?* Have you ever actually contemplated your thoughts and feelings? If not, this is your opportunity. Please honestly answer the questionnaire below.

My Self Assessment Questionnaire	Yes	No	Need To Improve
Do I know who I am?			
Am I honest with myself about who I really am?			
When people see me, do they see godliness? Do they see money? Do they see career? Do they see vanity? Do they see all of my issues? Do they see my anger?			
Am I the same person both inwardly and outwardly?			
Do I enjoy my life?			
Am I living in my purpose?			
Am I happy?			
Do I love myself?			

In admitting your need for assessment, you are agreeing to let go of everything you think you know to get back to a place of openness. It can be a grueling process. Often, when you come to this place it means you feel some sort of emptiness or lack of authenticity. Maybe you're not necessarily living a lie, but it's clear something is missing and you're desperate to get it back. It's possible that in these times you have forgotten the very essence of your being, your creator.

Our unwillingness to step outside of our pride and false identity hinders others from finding freedom for themselves. We pressure each other into putting on heavy foundations that hinder us all from experiencing true freedom and joy in our identity. We need pure, light foundations that tell the truth of who we are.

There are people who have come across Christians, spiritual people, churchgoers, and have even come through church doors looking for something that words could not explain. They were unable to approach an average person and say, "Yes, that's the something I am looking for!" Many people experience a deep longing for healing and fulfillment. It's like an itch that nothing else can scratch. They don't know what it is, but they are in pursuit of it. It is that "something" that could potentially change their lives at any given moment. Many of them left the presence of God-fearing people disappointed. Some are reading now, disappointed. When we are buried under the weight of life's burdens, we look to those who seem to have it together for guidance.

A person who has never been introduced to God

doesn't know that they need to look for Him. They find themselves mingling with God's people, listening for words of affirmation, strands of hope, and/or conversations that are mixed with love and peace. We all get lost under our heavy foundation; but no matter who you are, there is a better way to wear it.

Sunday in and Sunday out there are so many churched people sitting in the seats of the sanctuary with emotional complexities, spiritual idiosyncrasies, physical deformities, and mental vacancies, so much so that, when hungry people venture in looking for "something," they are met with false identities of people who should be the most loving and joyful around.

Tara was searching for hope and peace. Tired of hiding behind the person society had told her to be, she tried reading spiritual books, but she just didn't know how or what to change. As a last ditch effort, she decided to attend a service she had heard some coworkers talking about.

Tara's heart was open and she was desperate. The ushers seated her next to an older woman who had been a member for years. Tara was the first to speak and conducted a superficial conversation, just hoping the words she'd hear would be the "words of life" she desperately needed. Insecurely judging the young lady next to her, the older woman just made a comment about how short Tara's skirt was.

In that moment, Tara didn't see a woman willing to open up and love someone going through a hard time; she saw a woman who let her own self-righteousness and pride crush anyone in her path. Consequently, both women left feeling more discouraged than before. The older woman, hidden behind all of her issues and pain, bore a heavy foundation that caused her to turn inward while Tara was forced to go back to faking satisfaction with an unfulfilled life.

God needs us to be His extended hands. If we are too wrapped-up in ourselves, how can we help others? And if we spend our lives trying to hide the fact that we are unsatisfied with who we are (because it's really who we aren't), then the foundation will just become heavier and heavier. We must care enough about ourselves and about one another to not let expectations and a generic definition of beauty determine how we apply our foundation. We need to wear the shade for which we were primed; we need to be the person God has prepared us to be.

My Lipstick **Confession:** For as long as I could remember, I prided myself on being a strong and self-assured person. I was bossy at a young age. Those in my immediate circle called me a teacher's pet, a daddy's girl, and a goody-two-shoes. Through my efforts in life, school, and other areas of interest, I managed to attain some internal satisfaction from this persona I was haphazardly creating. Eventually, my personal treasure chest was filled with perfect test scores, awards, and other accolades. I bought into the hype.

I became this monster eager for more and was willing to take extreme measures to satisfy my hunger for accomplishments. My foundation was built on success. I was hiding behind an array of things I was capable of doing. But, in truth, I was lacking. I longed for someone to love the real me buried behind a plethora of insecurities. I presented the image that I was on top of it all, when in fact I felt very beneath it all.

The race for accomplishments was exhilarating at times, but it was short lived. I'd scratch something off of my bucket list and immediately be on to the next things. I was getting stuff done, but I wasn't enjoying any of it. The result was a physical, emotional, and mental exhaustion of energy that I can never get back. If I would have simply acknowledged my earnest desire for acceptance and love early on, I could have spent years growing in my purpose rather than focusing on pursuits that weren't necessarily part of God's plan.

A cycle is created when we believe that what we do will satisfy our need for love. We accomplish tasks, receive gratification from our peers, experience a temporary release, and then a void surfaces, so we go back and try to accomplish more things—and on and on. I hit my breaking point years later when I was overwhelmed with my children, managing my household, loving my husband, working in ministry, and constantly starting new projects. I didn't know why I kept adding more to my plate. I had no margins for anything else, yet I would create additional goals and would be overzealous to accomplish them.

I went away for a weekend retreat and God met me there. I realized that I didn't feel worthy of love without doing something for it. Over the years of my life, I started to see accomplishments as a way of garnering love that I feared I otherwise would not have received. It finally made sense why I was doing, doing, doing so much.

I received God's unconditional love for me. I learned to just sit and allow that same love to overtake me. I didn't have to teach Bible study or lead worship every Sunday to prove to God that I was worthy. I didn't have to stay up late making preparations for the school lunch or tidying up the house to communicate to my family that I was worthy. I accepted the fact that there was something broken in my life. I acknowledged that I could no longer function the way I was functioning. I allowed the process of introspection to prune those ways that weren't a part of who I really am.

Accomplishments don't bring true joy, contentment, and peace. Freedom comes when we realize we are loved, we are valued, we are good enough with or without those same accomplishments.

Thank God we are free.

Time to Reflect

> Before I formed you in the womb I knew
> you, before you were born I set you
> apart...
> —Jeremiah 1:5

At this moment, how do you really feel?

_____

_____

_____

_____

In one sentence write about an aspect of who you really are:

(Example: I am a funny person who genuinely loves people.)

_____

_____

_____

_____

Dear Lord,

You have known me since before I was even created. How did I manage to stray away from being exactly who you wanted me to be? I want to learn about what you have in store for my life. I want to live in your ways. Help me express the truth about how I feel and who I am. I want my persona to reflect godliness and genuineness. I know this will be a journey but I am willing to take the ride.

Amen

CAKED LAYERS

If I say we are hiding behind the lipstick, some women might disagree.

Oh no, I keep it real.

I can't stand fake women.

Oh, really? That seems strange considering we often convey an image of ourselves that is not founded in reality. We call ourselves fat when we are thin. We stare at ourselves in a mirror for hours yet claim that we are ugly. We spend ridiculous amounts of money on nice clothes, home furnishings, and cars. We recommend five-star establishments, talk about our love of fine wine, or give fashion advice on the latest trends and ignore deeper, more meaningful conversation about ourselves. As too much makeup will cause our faces to look caked and fake, layering on lies about ourselves and acting superficially will hide our most beautiful, genuine parts.

I remember meeting Dawn at an event some years ago. She was the life of the party—fun, and beautiful. She had an infectious, electrifying energy when she walked into a room. I thought I'd met a friend for life. I had visions of us riding in a convertible car around town, Thelma-and-Louise style.

We started hanging out and spending time together. Dawn's conversation was so superficial it was heartbreaking. It was like she was hollow on the inside. She learned how to project a certain persona in larger group settings but wasn't capable of having an intimate conversation about life.

Now, let me put this in perspective. During an entire conversation, a smile never left her face; her body language was open and inviting; she was engaged. It just felt as though she were reciting lines for an upcoming audition. She was portraying the character she thought people wanted to be around rather than her true self. I wanted to know how she grew up, what she was passionate about, what her biggest fear was. I asked, "Where do you see yourself in the future? When was the last time you laughed until you cried?" I wanted to know the person deep down inside, but her answers were fake and rehearsed.

Dawn wanted to talk about all the important people she'd been around, the designer shops she'd frequented, and what cars she'd been wanting to drive. She was living her life pretending to be something she wasn't. Unintentionally, Dawn set the tone for what the friendship would consist of: money, clothes, cars, and networking. It may not have been premeditated, but she was sending a message that friendship with her had limitations.

Every woman deserves to have a meaningful relationship with a person, not someone pretending to be something or someone else. Fakeness causes unnecessary pressure to build up around our relationships. When we are around someone who refuses to be vulnerable, that makes us put on more layers of our own for protection. What woman is going to yield her heart to someone who isn't offering the same? No one enjoys rejection or retribution for showing their true selves. When we let our guards down for one another, there is assurance that we are equally vulnerable and can trust in each other.

To hide something is to put it out of sight, to conceal for shelter or protection, to keep secret, or to hide the truth. To some extent we all hide. When we see things about ourselves that we don't like, we hide. When we hurt, we hide. When we miss the mark, we hide. When we are found in a state other than that which we would like to present, we hide. When life is not what we expect it to be, we withdraw our true essence and promote other aspects simply to protect ourselves from being mistreated or mishandled. We assume that by hiding we will never be hurt, not realizing that we hurt ourselves by missing out on the joys of being accepted with our flaws and all.

Sometimes we decide to withdraw deeper into an inner abyss, free from potential emotional threats. Initially we feel in control and shielded. But this existence has a false sense of safety because over time the part of us designed to connect and relate becomes hardened. Have you ever met someone like that? You engage in conversation but their responses are cold and closed off. It is likely that you are dealing with someone who decided not to feel anymore.

Sometimes we have sunk so deep within ourselves that we lose who we really are. The sad thing is that we didn't mean to sink. We long to be understood, loved, appreciated, and accepted. And we want more than anything for someone to know the "real" us. In schools, churches, and beauty salons around this world are women just like you and me still hiding behind caked layers.

Blotting Truth

What aspects of your life do you put out of sight? What parts of you are you trying to protect? We suffer through a substandard emotional human experience trying to cover up things that might make us look bad. We fail to realize that covering all those details keeps us from being who we really are. There are things we still carry that have been hidden since childhood. How can we expect to embrace things about ourselves that we have never acknowledged before? If we conceal our pain, we stifle our healing.

After a painful incident, many of us resolve that we will never be hurt in the same way again and do what we can to protect those inner chambers of our hearts from being exposed. We have taken the position that it is acceptable to give some of ourselves but never all. We engage in relationships only partially by listening to all of our girlfriends' problems without sharing any of our own. We are the first to offer advice, direction, and instruction but are equally unwilling to receive it. What are you concealing? What truth about yourself are you keeping a secret?

As a pastor's wife, I do not live a life absent of issues or personal flaws. The assumption that I do, often pressures me to show my stronger, more put-together side rather than my weaknesses. Over the years, I have found freedom after speaking about my flaws in conversations, sermons, and other interactions with people. It helps remind me of my own humanity and the necessity for growth in certain areas of my life. I even share things that happen in my life when no one is watching. It is healthy for us to be open about our weaknesses because doing so creates an opportunity for encouragement, help, and a deeper connection.

By not being open about our flaws, we perpetuate the desire to maintain a perfect image. We allow the people in our lives to have a skewed perspective of who we are and what our life is about, and then we wonder why our friends aren't there for us when we are going through a difficult time. How will they know you are struggling if you have never mentioned it before? Sometimes we don't show our flaws in our relationships because we are uncertain that the person will still love us if they know what is really going on.

Perhaps being afraid of rejection is a common reason for having defense mechanisms. We decide to hide the parts of us we aren't proud of—our flaws, struggles, and shortcomings. In fact, hiding seems to be a part of our nature. After Adam and Eve were deceived by the serpent and ate the fruit in the Garden of Eden, they hid themselves.

> Then the man and his wife heard the sound of the Lord God as he was walking in the garden in the cool of the day, and they hid from the Lord God among the trees of the garden. But the Lord God called to the man, "Where are you?" He answered, "I heard you in the garden, and I was afraid because I was naked; so I hid."
>
> —Genesis 3:8-10

We make a mistake, disobey God, ignore His will, and hide because we are so ashamed. We retreat. We cannot tolerate the feeling that we have missed the mark. Adam saw his nakedness and he hid. His sin took him far away from God. Our shame and feeling of failure does the same. We hide from people, God, and ourselves.

Much of our time is spent shielding and protecting what remains of our core being from those around us. We have allowed people and circumstances to hurt us so much that we withdraw deeper and deeper within. With every offense, a part of who we are is blotted out and can eventually be forgotten. When we are wounded deeply by someone, our response is to go back under our heavy foundation of false identity, pride, and vanity. All the while, we move further and further from the purpose of our true selves, which is to build relationships with one another.

Cheap Product

Have you ever opted for a cheaper makeup product, figuring it couldn't be much different from the high-end brands? I usually think I'm being very savvy until I get home and realize it takes twice as much of the cheaper product to even compare with the results of the expensive stuff. Despite this fact, I still find myself piling on drug store makeup morning in and morning out because a smaller investment is less painful in the moment.

Much like our investment in beauty products, friendship with other women requires us to choose how much time, energy, and other resources we are willing to spend. Sometimes true friendships seem unrealistic, so we continue engaging in very superficial ones for credibility's sake. We feel fake friendships are easier than real ones because they don't involve an uncomfortable degree of vulnerability, acceptance, or honesty. We don't have to worry about the answers to the questions: *What if she sees the real me and no longer likes me? What if I don't fit it? What if she hurts me? What if I reach out and she doesn't?* Imagining the answers to these questions petrifies us and we avoid taking the leap to start potentially long-lasting friendships. We expect others to reciprocate only what we want to give. In reality, quality relationships are not hard to come by, but it is our hurts from the past that keep us from forming them. Instead of facing possible confrontation and hurt from a genuine friendship, we prefer to hide behind superficiality.

Choosing shallowness in our relationships encourages others to do so as well. The results are communities of women who cannot show genuine love to one another because they have not opened themselves up to it. These relationships are cheap products that just can't get the job done. Sure, they cost you less on the front end, but they might be potentially harmful to you over time.

If we invest more in quality friendships, we stand the chance of getting hurt, but we also stand to gain freedom and joy like we've never had before. Genuine relationships are a mirror for the real us. If you wonder who you are, ask the people closest to you. They have a sense of your temperament, daily norms, and patterns that have been established over time. Openness creates opportunities for growth in areas of weakness, courage in the midst of lost perspective, and fellowship during good and bad times. It provides mutual understanding and fosters unconditional love. Having a shoulder to cry on and a safe place for honest dialogue is invaluable in a life full of ups and downs.

Strong female relationships are important in our lives if we are going to stop hiding behind the lipstick, and they don't end with our friendships. Sometimes we forget that the most influential relationships we will ever experience are with our family members.

When Erica was molested as a child, she was afraid and, on the advice of her mother, didn't do anything about it. Now, as a mature adult with children, she realizes her daughter is being molested. Rather than confronting it, she accepts it as a part of life, decides to move on, and pretends she doesn't see it. Truth be told, she really does not want to have anything to do with it. And so the cycle continues. Her daughter's voice is silenced by her mother's silenced voice. Because a relationship of care and protection has not been exercised through the tragedy of abuse, these women will continue to hurt one another and the cycle will continue.

We must begin to claim victory over the areas of our lives that could have an effect on the generations to come. Rather than telling our daughters what we did wrong, we need to tell them what is right. We expect them to do what we didn't do instead of giving them what we never had: the truth. We sow ideals in the hearts of young girls and base them on our mistakes—*all men are liars, don't trust anybody, you must look out solely for yourself or else you'll get hurt*—and what we wished we could have done, instead of relaying sound information.

The trouble with using our past experiences as the sole source of shared values is that our pain has a numbing effect. If we allow our circumstances to have the victory over us, we become slaves to our own bitterness, anxiety, and shame. Instead of turning to truth, we accept lies that have been skewed by our pain to look like truth. We turn to temporary pain relievers (money, sex, drugs, bitterness, violence, etc.) and dig even deeper into our damaged selves. In this state, we lose the ability to help or even engage with other people. Not only does this strain our relationship with our own children, it hinders their ability to engage in genuine relationships with other women who could bring a positive influence to their lives. We need to stop caking on the superficial and begin to engage in deep, lasting relationships with the women in our lives. It's time to tell the truth to one another and let go of our past pain, regret, and fear.

My Lipstick Confession: Being a pastor's wife can be a tough job at times. When there is a crisis in my life, I don't always know how to deal with it or navigate through it. In my early years, I thought vulnerability was a form of weakness. So when I was going through a difficult season, I would always want to hide. I would say, "If I could just crawl under a rock for a few weeks that will give me time to get it together." My number one inclination was to run for cover so no one could see me out of sorts.

Now I realize that when I am seen in an uncomfortable state, it allows God to be glorified. People get to see a realistic side of me, and it allows me to put on display the actions taken in a painful situation. By bringing pain and difficulty to the light, we gain victory over any darkness that might be crouched in the shadows of our past just waiting to consume us.

Time to Reflect

> "Who can hide in secret places so that I
> cannot see them?" declares the Lord.
> —Jeremiah 23:24

What aspects of your life do you put out of sight? What parts of you are you trying to protect?

_____

_____

_____

_____

_____

_____

Write about a situation when you said, "I will never be hurt like that again!"

_____

_____

_____

_____

_____

Dear Lord,

When there is a storm or painful situation in my life, why do I always hide? Hiding does not benefit anyone, and it even hurts me. It simply prolongs my pain. Help me to stand boldly in the face of adversity. I want to run to you rather than away from you. I know you are always there with your hand outstretched to receive me. I love you.

Amen

A "Beautiful" Routine

Every morning, no matter what's going on, we sit at the mirror and get ready. Even if we wake up on the wrong side of the bed and don't get to do anything else, we will at least put on some makeup.

When looking in the mirror, we may not like what we see. We may feel ugly, thinking our hair is thin and brittle, believing our nose is too wide. But we still put on lipstick and go to work. It might be all over our teeth, yet our smile will still be brighter when wearing that "good ol' faithful lipstick."

Some of us may not leave the house unless our faces are completely done up. Perhaps we subconsciously feel as though the makeup covers our insecurities. Maybe we feel that our foundation will cover up the negative thoughts we have and the mistakes we have made. And for reasons I can barely fathom, some of us won't even go to the kitchen without at least three shades of eye shadow on.

With makeup being such a secure and comfortable buffer between ourselves and the potentially harmful comments of others, intimate settings like women's retreats are difficult. Think about it: someone in the room might see us without our face on!

Are you the last to go to bed and the first to wake up just to preserve your image of beauty? To some extent, society and pop culture have shaped us to believe that we are prettier when we have these accents and extras, but let me give you the truth: wearing makeup has never been the issue. Even when the mascara is flawless and your lips are lusciously glossed, the question that remains, Are you presenting your true self?

Daily Cleanser

> Wash away all my iniquity and cleanse
> me from my sin...Cleanse me with hyssop,
> and I will be clean; wash me, and I will be
> whiter than snow.
> —Psalm 51:2-7

Those who often wear makeup know that your face should be clean before applying it. This process paints a vivid parallel to spiritual realities we face daily. Many of us use a deep facial cleanser before applying makeup. It is invigorating and eye opening. Cleansing is vital to removing impurities and dirt from our face.

We also need an emotional and spiritual daily cleanser. It begins with a block of time where we can be comfortable seeing ourselves for who we are, change our mindset, and recalibrate before we venture out into the many roles we play each day.

Each morning at half-past six, I am awakened by my nifty iPhone alarm. The atmosphere of my home is still and peaceful. I am certain to have no more than thirty minutes to myself before making breakfast, dressing my three school-age children, packing lunches, and darting them off to school. I do not look at the number of likes on my Instagram or check my email. I am not quick to turn on the news to see the happenings of the world. These moments alone are precious and vital to the start of my day. I spend them in reflection, in prayer, reading my Bible, and searching my heart.

Life can be deceiving at times. It can lead us to believe that we should be happy in the hustle and bustle of our exciting peaks or depressed in the valley of defeat. Taking time in the day to reflect on who you are, what you feel, and where you are going is invaluable. A quiet area free of distractions is imperative to staying in touch with yourself, your mood, and your overall emotional status.

What I find most important about my quiet time is talking with God in prayer about any worries or fears I might have. I am comforted and motivated by scriptures that remind me of His plan and promises for my life. It grounds me and allows me to feel in tune with myself as a human being and with my Creator. Our roles and responsibilities and the daily pressures of life, if not in balance, can cover up our true selves. Fight for yourself by carving out a small amount of time each day, uninterrupted, to "cleanse" away all the expectations, hurts, frustrations, lack of motivation, and the cares of yesterday.

When we become a child of God, He takes away all of our impurities and washes us with His very hand. If our roles and responsibilities begin to cover our foremost identity as His child, He is right there with fragrant soap and a soft cleansing cloth, ready to remind us.

It seems God wants to see our true selves. He wants to bring us out from underneath the heavily applied cosmetics of insecurity, expectation, and disappointment. These painted-on masks of obscurity cause us to trust in our false selves rather than our true selves.

Why do women start wearing makeup in the first place? Perhaps we begin by watching our mothers and then play with it on our own once they're not looking. As we grow older, we feel inadequate without it or we want to look older (or younger). Ultimately the goal is to gain something by covering up some flaw that gives us away or shows our imperfection or lack of experience. We do the same thing with our identities. We talk a different way to get attention, fit in with the crowd, or to obtain authority. We take on more than we can handle to prove that we are able. We abandon the things that bring us joy or fulfillment and comply with the status quo because chasing our dreams is just immature and might make us look foolish.

Whatever shade of lipstick we choose to hide behind, even if it matches our skin tone, God wants to wipe away. He wants to show us we are lovable without all the effort we put into making ourselves so or guarding ourselves from not being so.

Many of us have never received authentic love. Therefore, the idea of being vulnerable enough to expose ourselves to potential rejection is terrifying. I get it. Being vulnerable[2] is being capable of, or susceptible to, being wounded or hurt—open to moral attack or criticism. One of the most difficult things one can do is open themselves up to potential hurt. For this reason, the value of vulnerability is sometimes minimized with acknowledgment of the risk. Nevertheless, we cannot continue living lives based on falsehoods about ourselves. One way or another, we must come clean.

The Moisturizer

Our skin will look dry and flaky if we try to apply foundation or powder before moisturizing. A smooth, nourished surface is necessary to ensure that overlying layers are evenly spread. Moisturizer adds another benefit to our "beautiful" routine: It makes our skin touchable.

At our most open state we become a clear channel through which love and grace can flow. We love freely and unconditionally when our hearts are soft and true to the compassionate nature God has called us to exhibit. The only way to engage in long-lasting and meaningful relationships is to metaphorically moisturize our hearts. To make ourselves receptive of an unconditional love, we must condition our own hearts with an unconditional love of others. One of the reasons we resist vulnerability is to protect ourselves from the rejection of love from another, but what if we chose not to fear rejection and even love those who do reject us. (That is unconditional love at its finest.)

Maybe you haven't served well in the "turning the other cheek" ministry. Maybe the world has been intolerant or misunderstanding of you. From your moisture-deprived perspective, kindness is often mistaken for weakness.

Are you using toner instead of moisturizer? Toner, applied in our daily makeup process, helps to close our pores. In a sense, toner toughens us up to resist dirt and grime. However, it may also strip our skin of natural oils that we need to keep it hydrated.

Toner seems like a safeguard against the dirt that has been washed away; but really it is used as insurance, in case our cleanser didn't get the job done, and in place of moisturizer, if we would rather feel extra clean and safe rather than soft and touchable. The problem with toner is that it dries us out. When that happens, our skin begins to produce excess oils to compensate for the lack of moisture. Similarly, when we don't trust in God to cleanse us and don't open our hearts to be softened, we strip ourselves of true healing. Rather than relying on His love and allowing it to flow through us, we rely on our own abilities and emotions to flow out of us and pour all over people. The problem is that those emotions are not constant. Even if we weren't as bad as when He cleansed us, we still can't rely on ourselves. We may have eliminated the potty mouth, but are we still saying negative things all the time? We may be "yes, dear-ing" our husbands at every turn, but, what are we saying in our hearts? Perhaps we are the life of the party; but, are we still unwilling to go deeper in our friendships?

At this stage, comfort sets in and we are content with the strides made in our lives. Our pores may look smaller temporarily, but beneath the surface are the oil glands just waiting to burst open. Life progresses and trials make it more difficult to get through. Blemishes may pop up. We try to rid ourselves of them or cover them with even more makeup, but eventually our skin begins to scar.

Scarring eventually makes us hard in places that were once open. Sometimes the mistakes we've made or the circumstances we've found ourselves in initiate or add to this hardening. Maybe the loss of a job or home made us feel shame, so we hid it from everyone. Maybe we used toner to hide the truth of our pain instead of moisturizer to soften our hearts toward the pain of those we could potentially relate to.

Fear has the ability to change our perspective. It shows us what we are willing to lose and what we will not let go of. If you look in the mirror and see a dry, hardened person where there used to be a joyful, vibrant person, then it's possible you have chosen toner. Despite all of your efforts, you still don't feel you are enough and you still aren't the person you know you should be. You were so caught up in keeping yourself hidden that you became too afraid to let even the good parts of yourself be seen.

Remember when I said God is waiting with fragrant soap? Well, now is your chance. Start over with your "beautiful" routine. And this time, be sure to choose the moisturizer!

Concealed but Not Healed

> But now he has reconciled you by Christ's
> physical body through death to present
> you holy in his sight, without blemish and
> free from accusation.
> —Colossians 1:22

Even after we have cleansed and moisturized, blemishes

may still appear—those pesky little flaws that never seem to go away. Sometimes, instead of waiting patiently for them to take their course and disappear (or instead of learning to live with them), we purchase concealer. When we see something we don't like about ourselves in the mirror, we try our best to fix it. Whether it's the one hair we had to tweeze or the pimple we had to crush, our flaws must be hidden. We become experts at the cover up. Instead of seeing God's beautiful creation, we see what we are NOT, and we want to change it.

We hate the dark circles around our eyes and those "fine lines" because we see ourselves as not enough—as less than. Our favorite part of the application of makeup is when we get to play "the perfector." Concealer is a powerful substance that is designed to hide imperfections, blemishes, fine lines, and wrinkles. Its sole purpose is to mask areas that we feel aren't pleasing to the eye.

In life, we do the same thing. Circumstances can cloud our perspective to the point that we no longer believe what God says about us. The subtle imperfections that were brushed over with love become unacceptable to live with. We see blemishes when He says we have none. We see dirt when He says we are clean. We see darkness when He says there is light. We see worthlessness when He says we're worthy.

Some of our stories are a series of elaborate cover-ups with so much brokenness underneath. We cover up things that are not acceptable to us. We aim for perfection and the absence of fault. By doing this we prevent the very essence of who we are from being seen.

A failed marriage is a blemish, so we would rather allow our husband to cheat on us and let him do whatever he wants while we pretend like everything is perfect. We cover up our dysfunction so the people around will assume we have the picture-perfect life. If we sleep around and get pregnant, we can always fix it. Never mind the fact that ridding yourself of your unborn child might affect you mentally and spiritually. No one would ever know, and that is all that matters.

Some of us are so angry because of the way our lives turned out, but we continue to smile and offer encouragement to others so no one will ever know our true bitterness and disappointment. We conceal truth about who we are, not just what we have done. We all have made mistakes. We all are going through life with the face we want people to see, so, naturally, we conceal everything we don't want seen. We live a paradoxical life. We pretend we're okay when we're really not, and we work tirelessly to play a role.

> I am only 19 years old. I have a brand new Lexus, $800 purses, shoes everywhere, clothes, but what am I really worth?

I find it hard to comprehend the pressure that must be felt by women who continually spend money to buy things they cannot afford to support the image of "having money." Is it too hard for these women to be open with their friends and say, "I am struggling"? We force ourselves into invisible confines with the assumption that if we don't keep doing a particular thing, people in our lives won't love us anymore.

Have you ever met the woman who covers her

insecurity by being overly confident? She probably doesn't really believe her own boasts about herself. She wonders if she is enough to keep her husband satisfied, her friends engaged, and her career stable. Rather than conveying this, however, she prefers to speak highly of a great marriage, wonderful friends, and bustling career (which she may or may not possess). Her sleep at night is interrupted because she is obsessed with the possibility of losing it all. All of these emotions she must carry alone because she doesn't want anyone to feel she is weak. What an awfully lonely way to live.

Concealing truth burdens me because I have spent many days sharing stories and getting to know women only to find I was simply getting to know the "role" they were playing. I was desperate to know the person, not who they projected themselves to be.

I am reminded of Mrs. Johnson. She was a mature woman, probably in her late fifties. Spending most of her time in church and reading the scriptures, she had a reputation for being highly spiritual and very disciplined. Her profound ability to govern herself sexually for many years, or so she boasted, drew the interest of the younger women. They sought her counsel and wisdom for how they should live purely for God as single women. The biggest challenge with Mrs. Johnson was that she was sleeping with a number of men, all while playing the holier-than-thou role. But she was unwilling to lose the satisfaction that came from people looking up to her. Other single women looked to her great example without knowing that it was merely a cover. They noted the standard and commitment kept in their presence. However, what they saw was a role; she was living a different life behind closed doors. Meanwhile, there were young girls watching this seemingly ideal example and struggling, wondering why they had so much trouble abstaining.

The point is not that there are struggles; it is that you deceive yourself and others when you pretend the struggles are not real. It is okay to confront the truth and admit that there are things you are working through. Those things make you an even stronger witness later on.

It is time for us to throw away the concealer. Let's align ourselves with who we are and with the truth: concealing doesn't bring healing. It will save us many years of frustration by being truthful and honest. No more hiding. It is like a burden lifted when we realize that we are not perfect and, more important, no one has the right to expect us to be. Don't cover your imperfections. Learn to live with them and grow from them and you'll be an even stronger, more secure person once they do go away. Take the concealer off, take whatever comes, and let yourself heal.

Subtle Shades
Let's be honest. Sometimes makeup is just fun to wear. There's no harm in highlighting our stellar cheekbones, trying out a different shade of eyeliner, or popping on a new brand of lipstick. Part of the fun of being a woman is experimenting with new looks that compliment our naturally beautiful faces.

Nevertheless, after the work that has gone into cleansing and moisturizing, it would be a shame to make ourselves completely unrecognizable. The purpose of makeup is to enhance our existing features, not hide them. The same can be said of our lives. When we take too much upon ourselves, we are in danger of stifling our natural gifts and abilities—the things that make us unique.

We hide ourselves. But, why? Among a plethora of reasons, we hide because we are afraid of being vulnerable with others. The cost of authentic relationships and openness may not be worth the emotional expense. We say, "We have always been a certain way, so why change now?" Maybe we have been hurt before and decided that in order to protect ourselves we must cut everyone off. We live very guarded lives. We will open up only to a certain degree. We have let our guard down and have been disappointed by the way we were treated in the past. We hide because we like to be in control of our emotions.

We hide our true nature because we don't want anyone to have access to our deep feelings. It is the fear of releasing control that inhibits our progress. That release is the deal breaker. To be upfront and connect with other people means that someone has the opportunity to hurt us again. We consider the areas where we have been hurt before. We are saving it, being ourselves, for later when we settle down. After all, when you consider the odds, they could leave you like daddy did or could compare you to other women like your ex-husband. Some may even terminate you like your first boss. I have heard women say they just can't put up with emotional baggage and heaviness, deciding that relationships and their benefits (no matter how promising or enticing) are just not worth it.

It is uncomfortable to have people in our lives who affect us deeply and know our true selves. So, we continue to hide our true nature behind men, sex, clothes, accomplishments, and money while we slowly die inside.

> "I've got jokes, and people seem to like me for it. I might be hurting inside, but I'll keep people laughing because I'm too afraid of being rejected."

Others want to connect with you, but perhaps "you" don't exist. You have morphed from whatever pleased your father to whatever pleased your friends, your husband, and now to what pleases your children. Somehow, the opinions of others have dominated your life and caused you to live according to their expectations. It is perfectly normal to be a great mom or a doting wife, but when those roles overshadow your own worth and internal satisfaction, then it enters into dangerous territory.

You can be everything to everyone and give nothing to yourself. The soccer mom who sacrificed years of her life volunteering as a room mom, doing homework, and planning play dates also had dreams of writing a book or desired to have a Friday evening with friends. She, over the years, received so much validation from her husband, that her worth became attached to what she did for her family rather than who she was as a person. Her purpose and passions were suspended, or even lost, in the performance of a role.

Our honesty is time-sensitive. We say life is tough right now, so it's not a good time for change, right? We desire to be something that we really are not, so we create the person that is everything we wish we could be. Take off the extra layers of makeup that keep your God-given glow from coming through. You will never be a better version of yourself than when you are just being yourself. If something is keeping you from that, then it's time to stop and reevaluate. It's hard to let go of things we think have defined us for so long, but it's necessary if we are going to stop *Hiding Behind the Lipstick*.

My Lipstick Confession: I am a naturally strong-willed person. As a child, I covered up my emotions because I was the "strong child." Crying in front of others became a sign of weakness for me. I would hide behind my perceived strength. I always had things "under control" and did not want to disappoint anyone by not having it together. I still cried, but I would not allow others to see me. Years into my adulthood I had to start the process of reversing some of these behaviors. My strength is not confined to my ability to hold back tears. I realized being sensitive is a good thing. It is a sign that I am human and that I hurt like everyone else. There are places in our hearts that need further examination. Start the journey of self-exploration and discover the person deep down inside. Make the conscious choice to reveal more and more of yourself each day. By doing this, you have far more to gain than what you stand to lose. Give others the opportunity to know and love the real you. No more hiding. When you die, you will want people to have actually known the person that lived.

Time to Reflect

If we confess our sins, he is faithful and just and will forgive us our sins and purify us from all unrighteousness.

—1 John 1:9

Why have you been hiding?

_____

_____

_____

_____

_____

Write about a situation when you tried to "fix it."

_____

_____

_____

_____

_____

Dear Lord,

You are in ultimate control and I am not. Help me to make better choices when I win and even when I lose. I want to trust you in circumstances beyond my control and not try to fix everything. What you think of me is more important than what others say about me. I want to take my mask off and live free.

Amen

Face of the day

Just as using makeup to try a new look can be fun, trying out a new aspect of our persona can help us discover part of ourselves we haven't explored. But, we've also discussed the danger of getting too caught up in hiding our natural beauty under extra layers of bad decisions, overachievement, money—you name it. And we've talked about God's desire to cleanse and moisturize us. Now, let's look more into the reason for our "beautiful" routine.

A common term used by beauty bloggers and girls sharing makeup tips on Pinterest and Instagram is "face of the day." This refers to an image they have taken of themselves showcasing their cosmetic handiwork. Clearly, these women have put time and effort into making themselves look the way they do, and they want the world to see this image—one they single-handedly created.

So, what's your face of the day? What is the version of yourself you have created for the world to see?

Career Look

Does your pride and confidence stem from the letters behind your name? Do you tend to immerse yourself in the pursuit of continued education and upward mobility?

There is nothing wrong with being driven. If accomplishments have a lasting value to your life, that will probably land you the job of your dreams and a nice salary. But, perhaps, when it is time to relax and hang out with friends, somehow the conversation is dominated by all of your accomplishments and your new phase in the journey up the corporate ladder. Those things are very nice and worth celebrating, but who are you? What do you have to show for your life outside of your education and career? Are you truly happy, or is this just a cover up so those around you won't see that you are actually trying to win your daddy's approval? Maybe you finally feel worth something after being given up for adoption. Maybe you are trying to silence the voices in your head saying you are not good enough.

Ask yourself this: When does it end? At what point will you have "achieved" something? Will your all-nighters spent writing papers and studying for tests end with that diploma? Will your late nights and missed family functions end with that job promotion? Do you think that the life you are living now is not the life you hoped for? Do you keep pushing the limits of your relationships, your finances, and your own body just to be able to say you've "finally made it"? Are you driven in your work in order to avoid the realities of your personal life? Are you bent on climbing the corporate ladder to prove things to people who are no longer in your life?

It is amazing how our coveted careers consume our lives and become our primary source of happiness. When it seems the company is downsizing, you are thrown into an emotional frenzy and sent into depression. Anything that affects you so deeply may indicate something is out of balance in your life. You have allowed what was meant to be a contribution of passion and expertise to the world to be the breath that fills your lungs. It is healthy to have a reasonable amount of ambition, find a career that highlights what you are good at, and thrive in your position. But when that job consumes you to the point that you, your friends, and colleagues no longer recognize the real you, it has transitioned to the danger zone.

After our fifth grade class trip to Camp High Hill, I had an eye opening experience. I looked in the mirror and believed I wasn't pretty. My skin was very dark because we'd been in the sun and my hair was no longer finished like when I've just hopped out of the salon chair. It was drawn up and platted into braids after swimming. I vividly remember telling myself that I was never going to be pretty and that I should not expect boys to be attracted to me. I made a vow to myself at that moment: If I couldn't be prettier than any of the other girls, then I would definitely be smarter.

As I grew up, the best grades were simply trying to satisfy the void of acceptance and the self-worth that was somehow damaged by the rejection of others. I was on a mission to prove that I was good enough. I wanted to show the guys who rejected me that I would be much smarter than any of the "pretty girls" they'd ever date.

Whether in schoolwork or your upwardly mobile career, you can find yourself proving things to people who are no longer in your life. Perhaps you are getting more degrees just to validate that you have arrived or are now living in a world different from where you were raised. No matter how hard you work, you will only receive the satisfaction your heart longs for by being celebrated for who you are and not what you have accomplished.

Wearing the career look can be dangerous because you get so accustomed to the reward of the performance that you forget about the person deep down inside. It starts to feel better to achieve than to actually receive. Rocking this look long term can result in you being very successful but feeling empty and alone.

Sex Look

She couldn't help it. It radiated from her being. She had the flirty energy of a woman longing for the pleasure of a man. The look of enticement remained on her face and exuded from her being. It didn't matter the type of man or his social status. She was on a quest to scratch an itch deeply embedded in her soul. The number of her partners grew at the same rate as the hole in her heart. She had decided at the age of twelve that no man would take anything sexual from her again. Rather than dealing with the emotional pain of being molested, she decided to get lost in sexual behavior and to regain her control by giving it away instead of having it stolen from her.

Sex is a cover up for so many things: the desire for the attention of an absentee father, the need for love and affection, the fear of being rejected, or even the need to please others in order to be liked. The woman using sex as a weapon is treading on dangerous ground. This behavior can hasten the loss of self-worth.

Are you sporting the sex look? Perhaps you are so wrapped up in a man that you no longer can see yourself. If we are looking for you, we have to ask him to roll over. When your look is for a man, you are in for a lifetime of hurt. Maybe there is some personal satisfaction in knowing that you can make yourself appealing to the opposite sex, but at what cost? When the men in your life don't have to bring flowers, buy dinner, or even plan a night out on the town—in fact, your preferences and desires lead you straight to the bedroom—then you are cheating yourself out of a deep, genuine, and loving relationship that could be happening. Instead, you figure sex is all that men want from you, so you might as well just give it to them.

With this poor understanding and an insatiable, lustful appetite, you have created a portal to your soul. This openness makes you feel deprived if a man is not somewhere nearby. For you, sex is interchangeable with intimacy, leaving you feeling that you have to have a man in your bed every night. It's all you think about, all you dream about. You may just want to be loved, valued, and appreciated; but when you look for that in a man, every fling will end in disappointment.

Sex is one of the most intimate and precious activities one can engage in with someone else. We must see our bodies as a valued treasure. Would you give away a diamond worth 25 million dollars to someone you just met? Okay, maybe it is unrealistic to identify with such a rare jewel. Would you give away 500 dollars to someone you just met? Probably not. Yet, would you allow a man who bought you a five-dollar drink access to the most precious part of your body? Think about this paradox.

I'll never forget when a girl around the age of thirteen approached me about the subject of sex. I was taken aback by her sweet and innocent disposition. She wondered what was so sacred about sex. She said, "Having sex isn't a big deal, right?" She and her friends were starting to hear about sex parties and she'd remembered something I said and wanted to talk to me. My heart was broken by the pressure she felt and by the condition of her current situation. I decided to answer candidly with an analogy. I asked if she would wear her best friend's underwear. She responded with disgust at the idea.

"Really," I asked, "if she took them off right now after a long day and gave them to you to put on, would you do it?"

"Absolutely not," she said.

If we wouldn't do that, then why would we allow someone to enter inside our most private places (especially if they have been inside of other women)? You have value. There is a cost to experience the most precious part of you.

Marriage Look

All little girls have dreams of getting married someday. Some of us play dress up in our mothers' old wedding gowns. Some of us act out our weddings with our dolls. Those of us who are more extreme might even have a binder full of wedding plans with the groom as the only missing component.

There is no shame in craving the excitement and joy of a marriage celebration. The union of two souls is a wonderful, magical experience for all involved. It's perfectly natural for women to desire a husband—someone who will (in theory) always love her for who she is. That is something worth dreaming about. But that's just it; it's a dream. Marriage can be a truly wonderful thing, but if we cover up all of the things about us that might ruin our chance at a happily ever after, then we are lying to ourselves and to that poor man who is falling in love with someone who doesn't really exist.

Are you that little girl with marriage fantasies imprinted in your mind? Is having a husband the necessary component to completing your lifelong pursuit of acceptance or fulfillment? Are you giving up personality traits and dreams that make you truly special in order to be someone's perfect future wife? If so, you're putting on a marriage face.

Allow the man of your dreams to love the real you. Changing your innate characteristics to be desirable will always end in disappointment. You will have to exist in a false reality in order to keep your marriage. I have seen this happen far too often. Some women have a very strong desire to get married. That desire will cause them to do things they never thought they would.

Everything you do and everything you say reflects your desire for a wedding. All your time is spent thinking about the dress, the bridesmaids, the cake, and the venue. But wait! Who is he? Where is he? The idea of being married is noble, but when it overtakes you to the point that you lose yourself in the process, it has gone too far. You are hiding behind it.

Name Brand Look

When people are in your presence, do they see you or all of your name brands? What do they hear when they're talking to you? Is it a list of purchases and prices? Your desire to acquire and wear name brands exceeds what is considered within reason. It has become a consuming part of your life. You enjoy what the brands represent—success, influence, money, and exclusivity.

We can appreciate a great fashion sense and what we work hard for, but what we have should not overshadow our beautiful traits. When all you are communicating is your overwhelming desire to shop, buy, or accumulate more name brand stuff, you are consuming.

Your friends constantly hear about the looks from the new spring collections, where something is being shipped from, or what you were able to successfully get your hands on through your most exclusive personal shopper. At times, we don't even realize what non-verbal cues we are sending. There is an unspoken pressure that rests on your shoulders to compete and to succeed, to be the best, to wear the best, and to have the best. It is easier to identify with a brand because you are unable to connect with your own identity. Who you are has been lost somewhere along life's journey. Rather than discovering and recovering, we choose to reflect the most expensive brands in fashion as a stamp of our worthiness.

A brand is the "name, term, design, symbol, or any other feature that identifies one seller's good or service as distinct from those of other sellers."[3] Historically, branding was used to differentiate one person's cattle from another.

A hot iron stamp was used to burn a distinctive symbol on the animal. It was subsequently used in business, marketing and advertising. Marketing executives are compensated well to ensure that you desire the brands they represent. There is nothing wrong with nice taste and having the means to own the best. The issue arises when you get lost in the process.

You have a brand. Your brand is the best brand in the world. When you leave your house, the most valuable article that you should represent is yourself.

> For everything in the world—the lust of the flesh, the lust of the eyes, and the pride of life—comes not from the Father but from the world.
>
> —1 John 2:16

Our material possessions are life consuming. What begins as a simple luxury quickly becomes a necessity for happiness. To be honest, the desire for things may temporarily silence our raging need for love. Shopping becomes fulfilling because it does not have to respond with "I love you." It provides an opportunity for us to engage in behaviors that are considered safe and that require a reasonable amount of effort. Retail therapy is shopping with the primary purpose of improving the buyer's mood or disposition.[4] Often seen in people during periods of depression or transition, it seems as if everyone needs retail therapy every now and then. The key phrase is "every now and then," and the thing to remember is that the high doesn't last. Shopping is not and should not be a daily necessity.

Shoes and purses are really popular comfort buys. *I really don't like myself and I am not satisfied, so I will buy more purses.* We have silently communicated that the more things we have the better we feel. Spending money that shouldn't be spent on stuff creates more problems and won't fill the void. We go to great lengths to remain on the cutting edge in our circle of friends. Our lights will get turned off, bills will be paid late, and no food will be in the refrigerator all because having a new purse or a pair of shoes has become the priority. We are willing to use candles to light our house rather than prioritize our bills, just to look nice. I'm sure if we peered into the lives of those whom we admire from a distance (those we are trying to emulate with our expenditures), we would be amazed by what the women with all those cute purses actually experience at home. Shopping is their outlet. It is the only activity that soothes the sores of their hearts. But I say again, it's temporary relief from a life of hurt; it's a self-perpetuating cycle that will never satisfy.

Hungry Look

Food is essential for our bodies to function and thrive. The challenge arises when we allow our emotional issues to influence our physical desires. We connect the hunger that is natural to our hunger for happiness.

Some of us hide behind our appetites. We continually eat to suppress the hurt or inadequacies we feel in life. Our excessive and unhealthy eating patterns result in body image disturbances, health issues, self-esteem issues, and, in some cases, financial strain. We allow one masked problem to snowball into an array of others. When we are lonely, we use food as our consolation. When we are hurting, food becomes our therapy. Your true self may be lost somewhere in the never-ending abyss of food.

After having my third child almost three years ago, I buried myself in food. Actually, my vice was cupcakes. When I saw a cupcake shop, I'd have to stop to try a couple new flavors. That wasn't the only thing. I would watch the cupcake shows on television and give my unhealthy desire more variety. I awoke one morning and asked my husband to go to the local bakery for a dozen of their delectable mini cupcakes with the buttercream icing and sprinkles on top. When I nursed my newborn baby every two hours through the night, I would eat a cupcake. When my friends and family made their way to my house to visit the newborn baby, I would kindly ask them to stop at the bakery to pick up an order of cupcakes.

At my six-week checkup, my obstetrician informed me that I was actually gaining weight and that I hadn't lost much of the fifty plus pounds I gained during pregnancy. It finally dawned on me that my obsession with cupcakes was causing me to gain weight that I should have been losing. That was hurtful to me. I was becoming a different person both physically and emotionally. I went to God with my sadness and I received enlightenment regarding my situation. Prior to my delivery, I was constantly on the go, busy with ministry, my family, music, and so on. After my third child was born, I didn't have all kinds of things vying for my time. It left a void within me. I filled the part of me that enjoyed being busy, being needed, and having so much to do with my cupcake indulgence.

Perhaps you have been or currently are where I was. You no longer have to hide behind food. You don't have to yield to the desires of your body. You can overcome them. I decided to do something about the weight I gained and lost over thirty pounds. The weight I lost was not only physical but emotional weight as well. I purged myself of those unhealthy thoughts and those unhealthy food items I had in my house.

In my mind, the cupcake shop became a prison. I determined that I didn't want to be in bondage to my appetite anymore. When I had the desire to overeat or feel better by eating after a discouraging day, I reminded myself of the plethora of emotions that would follow that choice.

You can take control of your weight loss and live free. You are fearfully and wonderfully made. Decide to focus on a single desire that is stronger than eating. When you get weak, think of that one desire and allow it to pull you back to a victorious place. Don't forget to spend time discovering the root issue for why you overeat. For some its genetic, for others it's an escape, a coping mechanism, or a medium of self-love. You will need to identify and root out those triggers for long-term success. If you have struggled over the years with loneliness and food has become your confidante and friend, you may need to overcome that emptiness by seeking real friendship. No matter how difficult it may seem, take it one day at a time and you will do it.

Damaged Goods Look

Maybe you hide behind the fact that you are "damaged

goods." Things have happened to you in the past—you've been wronged, you've made mistakes—and it seems life just dealt you a crummy hand, so you take on the look of a victim. You pack on dark shades of hate, bitterness, and regret. You line your lips with thick, venomous words. If you stay on the defensive, then nothing can touch you, right?

The Face of Abortion

Abortion is a common practice that is becoming more accepted by society every day, as "nearly half of all pregnancies among American women are unintended...nearly one-third of American women will have an abortion [by the age of forty-five]."[5] What used to be a taboo subject, and still is to some degree, is now discussed on TV, in books, in politics, on the news, and in daily conversation.

If you've had an abortion, the reason for it might have stemmed from the fear of being a parent, financial concerns regarding pregnancy and raising a child, pressure from a loved one, etc. Whether or not you still have regrets or mixed feelings about it is not the main issue. What is primarily important is the fact that it happened. There is nothing you can do to change, fix, or repair it. You must, however, deal with the emotions, regrets, and any other issues that have arisen since then.

I have met women from all walks of life with many different experiences concerning abortion. One that particularly arrested me was the story of someone close to me. She had an abortion. As a matter of fact, she had two. One day, she gently and honestly replayed the scene while I listened patiently. She described the cold, drab feeling of the waiting room and the flat affect of countless women anxiously anticipating the next number being called. As she sat, she reiterated why this decision was necessary, that everything would be fine and that she would move forward. She continued the self-talk that prompted her to remain, even though everything in her was desperate to run.

Once in the room, she recalled the last few moments: the flushed feeling of the medication in the intravenous line and then the sudden peace of sleep. She awakened in the recovery room with more than relief—she was filled with unexplainable emotions, and this began her chapter of pain. She was modestly religious, and she felt having a child without being married was far too embarrassing. Now in her twenties, she wonders if she will ever be able to get pregnant again. She wrestles with the "what ifs" regularly. Although it was years ago and life has gone on, she has never forgotten the two children that never got a chance in this world.

Maybe you see yourself somewhere in her story. Maybe this was more than a choice made in a moment of desperation. Maybe the relief you felt afterward was short lived. It is time to be free from it all.

You might say, *You just don't understand.* Well, I've cried with enough women and even talked a few off the ledge to have a sense of what you may be experiencing. There is life after abortion. God still has a plan for you. You can and will move forward from this. You can stop hiding behind this deeply embedded secret. It has been difficult for the people around you because they don't fully know the source of your pain. Let them love you to your place of purpose.

The hardest part of the healing process is actually dealing with what happened. No more blocking things out. No more pretending that it didn't happen. It did. Please be honest with yourself. You owe it to yourself. Please make a commitment to deal with it. It is time.

Because of the pain I felt for women who were dealing with abortion and abortion-related issues, I decided to create an environment of healing. One Wednesday night in January some years ago, our women's Bible study became a veritable threshing floor where women opened themselves up to be purged of their pain and secret suffering. We taught on reconciliation and restoration, and the women were encouraged to write the following statement:

I had_____ abortion(s).

Confession was critical. They named the child on a small yellow card. They were encouraged to make internal statements of peace. We completely blacked out the sanctuary and allowed them to bring their yellow cards to the pulpit. It was a powerful time of release, as many were ashamed and embarrassed to confess what happened. With every step toward the altar, more and more liberation was expressed and felt. Although the healing process varies from one woman to the next, it is imperative that it happens now. Life is waiting for us all.

The Face of Pain

When the threat of a painful situation is impending, we lose it. It is similar to bracing oneself before being rear-ended by a truck. We hide our true self behind the painful situations we have endured. We see devastation approaching, so we run for cover as though our past pain can protect us from any future pain. The lengths to which we will go to escape the grasp of a difficult situation are mind-boggling. Pain is a part of life. Not the best part of life, however, it is essential to our human experience.

No matter who we are or where we come from, pain will eventually find us. We all have painful reminders of our mistakes, disappointments, missed opportunities, physical injuries, abuse, and just plain old hardship. It hurts to wake up without the person you love, raise children that turn to drugs, search for employment each day to no avail, experience rejection from family members, be terminated after years on a job, and/or lose the house you worked so hard to obtain.

Each of us has the power to do something very courageous (although it requires a lot of strength and dedication). We can choose to deal with the pain. It is easier said than done, I know. But too often we have turned a temporary situation into a life sentence. What prisoner chooses to remain in jail after they are pronounced "not guilty"?

It hurts, but the pain will not go away if we don't face it. Some of us live with it so long that we trick ourselves into thinking it is part of our identity, but that's a lie. It is time to begin the process of removing the Band-Aids and allowing our wounds to heal. Our wounds show others that we have a story to tell, that life has been a journey, and that we have struggled too.

The pain we experience perfects us in ways we are

incapable of doing ourselves. Difficult circumstances exist to purify us and to burn away the destructive qualities that are not fruitful in our lives. We must learn to gain the most out of the things that almost kill us. It may seem impossible, but if we look at the healed scars of those around us, we will find inspiration from people overcoming painful situations every day.

The Face of Sexual Abuse

One of the most painful situations that a person has to endure is sexual abuse. I am so sorry if you were raped or molested. It breaks my heart to know that this continues to happen in households across the globe. What kind of person does this to a human being? It is unthinkable, unfathomable, and horrible. What happened when you were too young or unable to defend yourself was absolutely dreadful. No man or woman had the right to touch you in private places. No man or woman had the right to take your childhood. It is heart-wrenching to know that no one was there to protect you.

Time has passed and you are grown, but maybe life stopped after you were robbed of your innocence. You have never opened your heart to anyone. It has been difficult to trust, show emotion, to feel, to believe, and to enjoy life. You have simply existed and gone through the motions. Your anger and frustration has taken the place of true love. Maybe your life has been in a downward spiral of promiscuity, drinking, loose living, partying, and drugs ever since it happened. *What's wrong with that?*, you may ask. The problem is that your life is worth far more than what you have made it. We need the real you, free from shame, anger, distrust, regrets, and sadness. You are hidden somewhere within the memory of your abuse. It is time to come out.

Yes, it happened; but it is over. You are alive. You may never understand why. You may never get the apology you have been waiting for. The wretched person who abused you may never come to justice, as they should. But you don't have the power to change everything, and you let their evil rule over you with every poor, self-destructive decision you make. By living behind their crime you continue to give that person power to control you, to abuse you over and over again.

You have the power to change your future. You have the ability to make sound decisions from this moment forward. Take the power and use it to live the life you have dreamt of. You may be hurt in some way again, but that's the risk we all take in life. There is a purpose for your life far beyond what you have been able to conceptualize. It is very difficult, but stop hiding behind what happened or you will drive yourself crazy by constantly reliving it. As long as you stay where you are, you are missing out on life.

Rejected Look

When it comes to the areas of life in which we are confident, we unashamedly step out to conquer. However, we tend to neglect the aspects of ourselves that require additional assistance: the tender spots, the "no touch" zones, or the vulnerable places that reside deep in our souls. We gloss over our inability to handle and adequately deal with rejection in more ways than one. Rejection is being told "no" to things we feel we deserve or have earned. Sometimes rejection is the unspoken gesture "or lack thereof" that leaves us with a deep feeling of inadequacy.

Rejection is commonplace. It is an occurrence and resulting emotion that we all experience at times in life. This will never change. It is ongoing and will be recurring until the day we die. (Even then, you may feel rejected that a neighbor did not attend the funeral service.) We will never escape the very crucial reality that not everyone will value or like us. Since we cannot eradicate rejection, the feelings associated with it, or the consequences of it, we must learn how to overcome it.

We translate rejection to mean many things in our minds. Not getting the job translates to: *I am not good enough.* Being served divorce papers translates to: *I am not worth loving.* Not being selected to sing the solo translates to: *There are others much better than I am, so I have no talent.* Even in childhood, we remember not being picked to start the afternoon basketball game, not being asked to go to the prom, or not being asked to be a part of the student council. Regardless of the way we see or experience rejection, we must recognize it and deal with it in a healthy manner.

I remember singing everywhere I went as a child. It was a joyous and exuberant feeling for me. Standing in the backyard belting out some good (and some bad) notes was the highlight of my upbringing. It wasn't until high school that I began my "rejection tape recorder." I embedded the vivid scenes of people saying, "it's not that she can't sing; she just doesn't have an ear for music," into my mind. Not only did I hear this, I replayed it over and over again. I felt that I was not good enough to sing before anyone. My backyard stage instantly became my inward closet. I kept my notes, whether good or bad, to myself. It took years for me to finally confront the feelings and counteract them with positive reinforcement and, in most cases, the truth.

I will never forget the day that I muttered the words, "I don't believe I am good enough to sing." My mom looked at me in disbelief and said, "Of course you are." It was the first time I openly acknowledged the lie I believed. I accepted what others said about me and never questioned it. These feelings of rejection and not being good enough hurt me. These lies caused me to decline opportunities to sing. I didn't invest my time and energy perfecting my ability to sing because I felt it would be a waste of time.

I started to question what made me feel the way I did about my voice. I sorted through the pain I carried as of result of what I believed. With an invisible T-chart and pen, I put the things I truly believed on one side and the things that people said on the other side. I started to read in the Bible about the importance of singing, psalmists, and musicians, and I adopted the positive attitude God has about such things in His Word. I had a gift for sing-ing and had never properly embraced it. The positive far outweighed the negative. Soon the voices of those people and their opinions about me grew faint until they were essentially non-existent. I began to sing with more convic-tion and confidence and the rest was history.

It is of the utmost importance that we don't allow the

feeling of rejection to stifle our growth and future potential. Let that feeling remain exactly what it is, a transient emotion. God wants to replace our "Face of Rejection" with one of confidence and positivity. We may never be the best at something, but that doesn't mean we cannot have an impact on others by using the gifts we do have and should be willing to share.

Perfection Look

She's so perfect. You know those women, the ones who seem to have it all. They're smart, beautiful, charming, and completely put-together. We marvel at them, aspire to be like them, and then get down on ourselves for not being perfect too.

Some wear the look of perfection. They strive to have the ideal family structure, home, car, career, and happiest marriage. Underneath the makeup, however, there is usually a false sense of happiness. When our inner circle feels we have the "perfect" life, there is no room for flaws.

We all can appreciate people seeing us at our best, and maybe we are most comfortable showing our better side; however, this is not the truth of who we are. The truth is that no one is perfect. We all have bad days, weeks, months, and years. To never experience a weak moment is not natural and, therefore, not a genuine representation of yourself. I'm not saying we have an excuse to let ourselves go and blame everything on our "imperfect" state. What I am saying is that we need to give one another a break and realize that perfection is not desirable because it is not relatable.

If we want to connect with others, we need to give

up the look of perfection and own our areas of struggle. Genuine relationships are formed when we celebrate the good times together and help one another during the hard times. When we stop trying to appear perfect we create an opportunity to experience love from people who are familiar with our weaknesses. Sharing our weaknesses helps us to become more vulnerable. Being vulnerable fills a space in our hearts in ways that words cannot adequately describe. It is allowing ourselves to be open to advice, support, and encouragement in those areas we need it the most. It is difficult for the person who has everything to publicly receive something. When you wear the perfect look, the assumption is that you never need anything. So, when you are feeling pressured or saddened, there is no real place to go get help or mutual understanding. No one should be in such a discouraging and lonely place.

Wealthy Look

> Whœver loves money never has enough; whœver loves wealth is never satisfied with their income. This too is meaningless. As goods increase, so do those who consume them. And what benefit are they to the owners except to feast their eyes on them?
> —Ecclesiastes 5:10-11

When you wear the face of wealth, no one can see the real you because all they see is money. You see the checking account balance, and you instantly feel good about yourself. "You have arrived," you quietly utter to yourself. There is this assertion that "I am somebody now."

Money is creating that blanket you had as a child. When you are sad or hurt you feel comforted by the fact that you have money. Money solves everything for you. Either you are working five jobs to get more of it or you are restrictive and don't want people to come around because you are afraid they will try to use you for it. You hide behind the money. As long as you use your financial resources as your safeguard, the real you will always be a slave to it.

Who you are has nothing to do with the money you have. Money is necessary for the world to operate, but keep its importance in its proper place. Allow people to love *you*, not what you have the ability to do. I am more concerned with the person you are deep inside.

What is your Face of the Day?

Whatever your "Face of the Day" is, and we all have them, it is time to stop hiding behind our made-up looks and allow the core of our beings to be seen.

What are you hiding behind?

- Career
- Sex
- Marriage
- Name Brands
- Damaged Goods
- Rejection
- Perfection
- Wealth

It doesn't have to be limited to these. There are so many faces we put on each day. I encourage you to figure out what yours is. What issue has kept you bound? What has hindered your perspective? What has hampered your life? What happened to you? What do you see when you look in the mirror? What are you still hiding behind? Whatever it is, we are going to deal with it here and now. There is too much life to be lived. You have spent far too long wrestling with the same issues. Freedom is here and freedom is now. It dœsn't matter where you find yourself. It dœsn't matter how deep and dark the situation.

Maybe I am hiding and maybe I am not revealing my true self. But how do I get out?

Aha, now we come to it, the reason for our "beautiful" routine. Remember, you have been cleansed. That means all of your past hurts and failures are gone, expunged from the record. You are not what your mother said you were. You are not what that man called you. You are not doomed to a life of repeated disappointment and defeat. You have a choice. All the hiding you've been doing behind your career, your clothes, your anger, your pride, or your bank account can end.

I wrote earlier about choosing moisturizer over toner: moisturizer makes our surface soft and touchable while toner dries us out and may cause further blemishes and eventual scars. Now is the time to choose. Moisturizer or toner?

You are worthy. You are beautiful despite everything you've done or that has been done to you. You are not defined by what you can do but by who you are. Let go of the things you are chasing and choose to be softened, to be vulnerable. It doesn't feel safe, I know. It can be utterly terrifying, that's true. But it will be irrevocably beneficial to your growth, influence, and overall joy; this I promise.

My Lipstick Confession: My "Face of the Day" was a look of perfection. I was consumed with fixing the things about myself that I felt weren't "put-together." I was bothered by one pimple of my face, one hair that was out of place, or one wrinkle that wasn't ironed out of my shirt.

I wasted so much time fixated on "the one thing." You know, the one thing I don't like about my life: my shape, my skin, my ministry, my face, my hair, and you know the rest. I circumnavigated the ninety-nine percent that is right to zero in on the one thing that I considered wrong. Maybe this was a season that I really needed more moisturizer on my heart. I needed to revisit the fact that I was loved and perfect because of who I was and not because of the image I projected. Sometimes we all get stuck on what is seen on the outside rather than fixing the inside. I grew frustrated because the moment I fixed one thing, another would surface.

Eventually, I realized that I didn't want to spend precious moments of my life worried about "the one thing." I intentionally allowed my flaws to be seen, and a miracle happened. I was still myself, I was still loved, and I still had life. Forget the one thing. I have learned to stop getting hung up on what is not "perfect" by changing my perspective each day. I learned how to see the beauty in the complete picture and not zoom in on what I feel is out of place. Surprisingly, people didn't treat me any differently. Rather than fixing things, I now spend most of my time enjoying what is beautiful about me.

Time to Reflect

> Therefore, with minds that are alert and
> fully sober, set your hope on the grace
> to be brought to you when Jesus Christ is
> revealed at his coming.
> —1 Peter 1:13

What is "Your Face of the Day?" Why do you wear it?

_____

_____

Dear Lord,

Help me to embrace who I am deep down inside. I am tired of hiding behind things, feelings, and emotions. I want to freely express who You have created me to be. I am willing to do whatever it takes to free myself from all the issues I may have in life. Please help me rediscover who I really am.

Amen

MAKING UP

Healing is a process. It does not always happen "just like that." It won't happen with the snap of a finger. It will require trust and diligence. It takes time (especially when you have been raised to think that no one has the best intentions for you and that everyone is out to get you). When you have been indoctrinated to believe that everyone has motives, you will have to retrain your mind. All those thoughts and memories can't be wiped away instantaneously, but the sting of the past can be taken away.

You must roll up your sleeves and get to work. Truth is infectious, but first you have to want to be truthful. So much time and energy is spent perfecting stories and hiding things to secure our image, but an immediate benefit to your honesty will be the discovery of who you really are.

You must find the "you" minus all the trappings of success: the fine man, the clothes, the money, and the education. Where is the "you" that you remember before the rape, the hurt, or before mother died? The discovery of the person you repressed deep down inside is crucial. Pain has frozen us in time. We need to thaw and get to know the person begging to get out.

Everyone has the inner being that is radiant and hopeful. It is our discretion as to who we feel is worthy enough to meet her. However, it is crucial that we discover for ourselves who we really are. No more making up the person we want everyone to see. Finding "you" will be the best thing you could ever do.

How can I take off the mask and live free?
How can I stop pretending I am somebody else?
How can I accept all my frailties and weakness and show others?
How can I find the real me deep down inside?

Image Consultation

Sometimes, in order to understand how to best present our unique selves, we need to schedule an image consultation. The honest opinion of someone who views us objectively can teach us what type of clothes best fit our figure, which shade of lipstick best matches our skin tone, and which hairstyles are more flattering for our face shape. Whereas other relationships in our lives tend to be biased and make suggestions based on personal preferences, an image consultant uses their professional knowledge and impartiality to assess what looks are best for their client.

God is like an image consultant in our lives; but rather than merely being impartial in his assessment of us, He has created our unique identities and knows how we can best use our natural gifts. Just as we would seek an image consultant to teach us how to dress better, we can ask God to help resolve the issue of our mistaken identity. Through the Holy Spirit, God will reveal to us the root issues that hold us back from our identity. In prayer, we can talk to Him about where we are, what we long for, and where we are going in our lives.

He can cleanse us of all the impurities that keep our "true selves" covered by the unflattering faces of each day. Ask Him what His intentions were when He created you. Consult the Bible, our ultimate how-to guide.

Find what God has to say about you and then match your perspective to His. Speak His words until you believe them. Believe those words until they are manifested or become real. Be those words. Allow His Word to transform you from the inside out. Allow Him to help you get rid of all the junk. Allow the purity to flow and to restore your natural glow. God is more than willing to teach you how to get there if you'll just book a consultation.

Appearance Analysis

Once you have consulted God concerning your true identity, be prepared for an appearance analysis. This is the feedback that so many of us tend to ignore. You see, it's easy to ask God questions, but sometimes His responses are not what we had in mind. Ultimately, His work is meant to point us back to Himself. But that means that we cannot rely on ourselves, on our own "beautiful" routines that have become so familiar. We cannot be the "Face of the day" that we so badly want others to see. Instead, He will ask us to be the person He created us to be. His analysis will come back and the results will show that we look too much like the world and not enough like that person He lovingly created.

Receiving the truth about ourselves can be difficult. Honesty is not always the easiest route, but it is always the most beneficial in the end. If an image consultant assesses that you have a curvy figure when you, in fact, have an athletic build, then they will most likely put you in clothes that do not flatter. In a similar way, if you ask God about the purpose of your life and He responds by saying that it is to have the biggest house to impress your friends, then He would be giving you an ill-fitting outfit to wear.

Our core nature is not made up of material things. Within each of us is a desire for something deeper, something more spiritual. Because God is a good image consultant, He will not give us a faulty analysis. We can trust in His assessment of our very beings because He created our inmost person. He knit us together and knows exactly who we are even when we don't.

Regardless of how you feel, you are not alone. Someone cares for you, loves you, and appreciates you. This isn't a person who is concerned about you because of what you are able to do, nor does He ignore those who have made mistakes. He loves the *real* you, and He wants to help you see that. You might be uncomfortable with the way God views you at first (everyone is a little skeptical of pure, unadulterated affection), but be comforted by the words He has written across the top of your analysis: "For I know the plans I have for you...plans to prosper you and not to harm you, plans to give you hope and a future. Then you will call upon me and come and pray to me, and I will listen to you. You will seek me and find me when you seek me with all your heart. I will be found by you... and will bring you back from captivity." (Jeremiah 29:11-14)

Seek Him out. Ask the real questions: How did I get this way? Who am I? Why am I on this earth? What is my purpose? Spend some much needed quality time alone, particularly, away from "things" near and dear to you. Do some soul searching. Imagine yourself without the lipstick and deal with the emotions that arise.

If you listen to God and allow it, your appearance analysis will help you discover the essence of who you are, figure out what has meaning in your life, and learn what your purpose is.

Doing Makes the Difference
The "Real You" Analysis:

I enjoy _____

_____

My heart breaks when _____

_____

My biggest aspiration is to become _____

_____

If you came to my house at bedtime, I'd be wearing

_____

I would like to remembered for my _____

_____

If you knew the real me, you'd know that _____

_____

Cosmetic Surgery

> We cannot change our past. We cannot change the fact that people act in a certain way. We cannot change the inevitable. The only thing we can do is play on the one string we have, and that is our attitude.
> —Charles R. Swindoll

Sometimes women choose to change their appearance permanently. For whatever reason, millions of women undergo some sort of cosmetic procedure each year. What they may or may not realize before surgery is that the results are permanent.

In our lives, we cannot always change our circumstances. However, we can choose how we respond to them. Sometimes we are unaffected, sometimes we adapt and change for the better, and sometimes we harden ourselves and make choices that could leave even more permanent damage. Altering our personality to deal with difficult circumstances is like performing cosmetic surgery on our hearts. Though we might be able to find happiness later on, there are permanent consequences that result from the choices we make in this altered state.

Stacy was sick of seeing her husband come home late at night and leave for work early in the morning. She knew something was going on, but she couldn't prove it. So, she began searching his phone, checking his emails, and driving by his office. It was true. Her husband was cheating, and Stacy was devastated.

As time went on, Stacy's personality changed as her insecurities and fears got the better of her. Her children noticed the difference in their once loving, attentive mother who was now withdrawn and preoccupied. But honestly, Stacy didn't care. How could she? A cheating husband was her biggest fear, and now that fear was Stacy's reality. She promised herself that she wouldn't just keep forgiving her husband for the affairs he had with other women. She decided revenge was best for all the pain he caused her.

Stacy traded her Tuesday night book club meeting for the VIP section at an upscale Hollywood club. Her hurt blinded her as she continued to indulge in drinking and smoking with people she barely knew. This mother of three and doting wife was sinking fast. After partying one night, she didn't go home. She slept in the arms of another man. That one night created a hole in her soul that would never be filled. She went home empty and infected with herpes. Her choices had permanent consequences.

Making peace with your past is having the ability to relinquish the hostility toward events, hurts, disappointments, and poor choices that happened in the past. Develop the ability to remember painful circumstances while rejecting any erratic and self-destructive behavior or thought patterns that may arise. Face it head on. You cannot change anything about your past and nothing you do will fully allow you to gloss over it. Instead, you must overcome it.

You have no control over the past. Pause for a moment to accept that. It is over. It is done. You can take as many showers as you like and will not be able to reverse what has happened to you. Acknowledge it. Say it aloud, whatever it is.

"I was molested."

"My marriage failed."

"They did not want me."

Resolve that there is nothing you can do to fix those things. However, you do have power over the choices you make from this point forward. You determine your feelings. You set the trajectory now. Embrace the newness of life that is here today.

> Therefore if anyone is in Christ, he is a
> new creature; the old things passed away;
> behold, new things have come.
> —2 Corinthians 5:17 NASB

You can and will experience a fresh new start by embracing your past, present, and future rather than altering your self-perceived weakened areas. Instead of permanently changing the face you show people in your most vulnerable moments, change your mind about what those moments say about you. Instead of believing that no one loves you, believe that God does and share it. Instead of slipping into depression and bitterness over your failed marriage, celebrate a new sense of freedom from the pain your spouse was causing and pray for healing for you both. Rather than hiding your struggle with weight, schedule time to workout with other women dealing with the same issue.

Your pain and hurt and disappointment are not signs of weakness; they are a reflection of God's work in you. At times, it seems easier to gloss over hurtful memories or experiences, but they simply show others that you are still human. There are areas of my life that God is helping me through. It's like God puts "under-construction" tape around those painful places in my life. Those places don't make us look bad; they make us normal. Some of the things you have experienced were a part of a pruning process. Certain things had to be cut away in order for something more beautiful to bloom. Do not get frustrated when life does not seem to go your way or when it feels as though you just can't get ahead. It may very well be God's hand pruning you in order to make you more fruitful.

Doing Makes the Difference

My past was filled with _____

I cannot change that by changing _____

My heart was broken because _____

I saw life through the lenses of _____

I am _____ to begin the journey toward my freedom.

I accept what happened, but it will no longer stop me.

Write a Statement of Empowerment to help you move forward. (For example: I will no longer allow my parents' divorce to make me skeptical of my own marriage. Instead of pretending my husband can't affect me, I will tell him about my fear of our separation.)

_____

_____

_____

_____

_____

_____

Recovery

> Forgiveness is the fragrance that the violet
> sheds on the heel that has crushed it.
> —Mark Twain

We learned at the beginning of this book that God wants to use us, but He can't do it if He can't *see* us. When we lose ourselves to a permanently altered state, we can no longer serve Him as the person we were originally designed to be. However, this does not mean hope is lost. Unlike a physical cosmetic surgery, we are not stuck with an altered nature. While there may be some permanent consequences, God is able to restore our spirits to a full recovery. However, the cost of recovery is very great.

In order to return to the person who has been lost, we must be willing to forgive the people who have hurt us as well as ourselves. This will be the hardest thing you will ever have to do. Release those people, situations, and incidents. Release them. As long as you hold onto the past, you are unable to experience the freedom that you long for. You must completely forgive.

I'm not saying you should sit and have coffee with the person who robbed you of your childhood. Forgiveness is not letting your guard down and pretending bad things haven't happened. Forgiveness is the renunciation or cessation of resentment, indignation, or anger as a result of a perceived offence, disagreement, or mistake; or ceasing to demand punishment or restitution of yourself and of others. You must let go of the time you lost and the missed opportunities. You must release those who have hurt you and those whom you, yourself, have hurt.

Forgive the people who did not keep their promises to you. Fight to do this, it is absolutely necessary for your journey of healing and restoration to be successful.

And whenever you stand praying, forgive,
if you have anything against anyone, so
that your Father also who is in heaven
may forgive you your trespasses.
—Mark 11:25 ESV

My mom used to say that if you keep on living, you will go through hardship. At the tender age of eighteen, I laughed at the notion of hardship because I felt invincible. I was determined to make the right choices in life, those that would warrant some sort of religious pardon from pain. I was afraid of pain, heartbreak, and disappointment. I did not know how to brace myself for the blows of life that would somehow find my address and eventually invade my emotional fortress. After living a few more years and enduring those difficulties my mother promised I would endure, I learned that the hardest part wasn't experiencing the pain; it was finding the courage and the ability to let go and forgive. Yes, it is hard. But it is necessary for true healing.

I always had high expectations, which caused me to carry a lot of disappointment. I would plan a party for my birthday and invite all of my friends. When they didn't show up, I would be terribly sad and would hold a grudge against them for not being there for me. Initially, I decided to alter myself to have no expectations of anyone to do anything for me, but I missed out on spontaneous outings, good times, and happy memories. Instead, I became more vulnerable and forgave others for not measuring up to my standards. Many of my friends wouldn't even know why I stopped returning calls or hanging out when I held grudges. I held something against them that they did not even know about and lost my own joy in the process.

There have been some horrific things that have happened to us in life. Unspeakable things like molestation, abandonment from a parent, parental favoritism between siblings, divorce, having a child on drugs, felony convictions, the loss of a child or parent. These and other sources of pain have wounded the hearts of people everywhere. Sometimes we get through by blaming others. Sometimes we cope by putting on a face of hardness and apathy, and sometimes we just shrink away and avoid the world at all costs. Unless we respond to life's hurts with forgiveness, we will never recover true joy, enjoy meaningful relationships, or progress to wholeness.

Forgive those who have hurt you and, more important, forgive yourself. When we encourage forgiveness it is generally implied as an action toward someone else, however, many of us really struggle with forgiving ourselves. Those "what ifs," "whys," "I should haves," and "would have but didn't" kind of thoughts are the ones that hold us back. Maybe it was not being at the bedside of a dying mother, the child that was aborted, the degree that was never completed, or the adulterous relationship that lead to your unforgiving state. There is so much power behind releasing yourself from the myriad of emotions that hamper your progression in life.

Out With the Old

Life will have its ups and downs. We will have good days and bad days, good years and bad years, and over time the makeup we have been wearing will start to get old. Our mascara will get thick and clumpy, our blush will be missing a huge circular chunk in the middle of the compact, and our favorite shade of lipstick just won't look as good anymore. We could continue wearing our old makeup until it runs out, or we could go ahead and throw it out. Either way, the makeup eventually has to go.

The same is true in life when the mask has to come off and the truth has to come out. At some point, it is necessary to acknowledge the pain some issue has caused, recognize that there is nothing you can do about the wrong that was done to you (or that you did to someone else), and stop trying to hide behind whatever emotion or façade that makes you feel strong and safe and untouchable. Throw out that old makeup now because all it's doing is keeping people from seeing the real you—it's keeping you from experiencing healing and genuine relationships with others.

No matter how awful the circumstances were, there are still things you have learned along life's journey that no one can steal from you. You are made stronger by your weaknesses, not by the barriers you put up as a result of them. You have the potential to become a better person through it all, a person to whom others can look for encouragement and inspiration. See the possibilities waiting on the horizon for you. You cannot change anything in the past and certainly cannot prevent any hurt from happening in the future, but you can find freedom by forgiving and letting go. Replace that old makeup with a new, all-natural glow.

As we chart a new way of living, we need to be intentional about getting rid of our old way of thinking and functioning. We cannot continue doing the same things we used to do and expect to fully embrace our true selves. It is imperative that we do our very best to forge ahead without the same behaviors that kept us hiding in the first place. Fresh mindsets and new behaviors help strengthen our true selves.

Doing Makes the Difference
Throw Out the Makeup

Write a heartfelt letter to the person you are forgiving (even if it is yourself). Be as open and transparent as possible. Be clear about what you are forgiving them for and why you are forgiving them. After writing it, seal it in an envelope and tear it up. This is your symbolic way of "throwing out the makeup." Let go of the emotions you have been hiding behind and offer yourself or someone else vulnerable, unadulterated grace. For you, there will be no more "making up." Now is the time to get real with yourself and with those who have hurt you.

Taking Off the Lipstick

The final stage of our makeup routines normally involves applying our lipstick. This part of the process is important for the look we are going for. Normally, a bright, bold lip requires more than a proper application; it requires an attitude of ownership. When we own the look, we feel unstoppable. Nothing can hurt us as long as we have a daring color making our lips the first thing people notice. We reapply throughout the day because losing the lipstick might cause us to lose our control—you don't mess with a woman who can rock bright red lipstick! If we are stripped of our look, people might see a version of ourselves that is an open, easy target.

As I mentioned in chapter four, God wants to wipe away our lipstick. He wants us to surrender the power and control of our lives to Him so He might show Himself through us. Genuine relationship occurs when two people open up to one another without judgment and under no false pretenses. Wiping off our lipstick is God's way of helping us achieve this level of vulnerability. He strips away the makeup we are hiding behind and reveals us to others for the sake of relationship and encouragement.

Generally within the confines of family, friends, and confidantes exists some degree of love and trust. Just as when we lose our lipstick on the side of a coffee mug, when the circumstances of life invade these emotional safety zones and confront us with the reality of loss, we feel exposed.

Balm

We discussed in chapter three how superficial relationships are sometimes easier because we have to offer less of ourselves. Most of us are more willing to accept someone else's vulnerability than we are to offer our own. For this reason, it is easy to enter into a relationship with someone who will open up. The hard part, however, is letting go, because no matter how hard we try to avoid it, letting someone into our lives means we automatically give a part of ourselves away. We can keep our lipstick on and try to maintain control over the look we are presenting, but one way or another it will smudge. Whether it is the sudden passing of a child, the loss of a parent following a long battle with cancer, or the unfortunate divorce from a spouse after twenty years of marriage, it is hard to let go of relationships, and it affects us no matter what.

When times are great with our loved ones, we make beautiful memories that give us emotional satisfaction and enhance our overall sense of well-being. When times become challenging and the threat of loss is impending or even realized, those are the memories we must fight to recall. Those good memories are a balm for our exposed, dry lips. God gives us the good memories in our relationships to overpower the pain of loss. We shouldn't be afraid of losing control or of the pain that is present after suffering loss. Some have spent years hiding behind the lipstick after a tragic loss. Too often we choose the power-packed lipstick to complete our "Face of the Day" and ignore the soothing balm that will bring true healing. Remember, God does not want you to hide behind a made-up look. He wants to cleanse you and soften your hard outer shell. Instead of storing up fear and anger and bitterness in your heart, He wants you to store up even more love for even more people.

Maybe you have not found this balm yet. Perhaps you've instead found yourself taking on more at work and balancing a household. You pushed all the feelings into a back corner somewhere. Years later, you are calloused, unloving to your husband and family, feeling empty inside, and always searching.

I experienced loss in a profound way. Darren S. Rockett, my son's Godfather, was a great man. He was a father, son, community leader, firefighter, deacon, and friend. In the prime of his life, mid-forties, we enjoyed spending time together. Our families traveled the world together; we did ministry together and even endured hardship together. We spent some of our best moments planning for the future and reflecting on the road ahead. He was a joy to be around and had an impact on those his life touched.

One afternoon, after spending the day with my husband, friends, and his family, he retreated to his bedroom to rest. He suffered cardiac arrest in his sleep and eventually died. This vibrant, healthy father of four—a man devoted to saving lives, had now lost his own. It was absolutely devastating. It was the first time I had to explain to my five-year-old son that he wouldn't make his trip to the fire station, ride bikes through the neighborhood, or play catch with his beloved God-daddy. So many memories, so much potential, so much love and time spent building this relationship that was suddenly snatched away.

It was tempting to hide behind my face of perfection after this ordeal. No one had to know the emotional anguish I felt for our dear friend. It would have been easier to pretend nothing had happened—to stifle the pain of loss by never speaking of it or thinking about it. But God has provided a balm. We allow the memories to come, tears to fall, and life to continue.

We cannot escape the reality that the people we love and have become accustomed to having around will one day leave us. Sometimes we get time to prepare and other times we do not. The journey through grief and loss is difficult; but God gives us life that we may love and provides the balm when it's time to let go. Don't reapply your lipstick after a devastating blow. The world doesn't need to see your strength and ability to hide your pain; they do need to see someone who can feel and express the pain of loss and then let go.

Doing Makes the Difference

I need to let go of_____

_____

I really don't want to, but I know it is best.
Write this statement down on a small piece of paper. Think about what you are about to do. Let it fall from your hand into a place that it cannot be retrieved.

Skip the Gloss

We are often blindsided by what happens in life, yet we gloss over life's disappointments as if we expected them all along. We can only get out of this life what we put into it. Counteract pain with good. More positive thinking will drown out negative thinking. One step in the right direction is better than two steps in the wrong direction. Change your expectations of life. Rather than saying, "This will never change," say, "This season will pass." Find as much good as you possibly can around you without glossing over the bad. Expect your life to shift and to be full of meaning and purpose.

I am amazed by what women are able to accomplish. We can take care of the kids, go back to school, work full-time, be the soccer mom, team mom, room mom, and still start a business. We have the drive to accomplish goals and surpass the odds. Allow that same determination to spill over into our drive for a better human experience, reconciled thoughts and emotions, and meaningful relationships. We should earnestly desire peace, joy, love, patience and the fruits of the spirit. Change the expectation that everyone can't have a "good life" and that you must make lemonade out of lemons. We convince ourselves that we need to do the best with the cards we are dealt in life. This causes us to live way beneath what is readily accessible to us.

I remember feeling down about a situation in my life. I needed to make a crucial decision that would ultimately affect my future. During that time, I agreed to go on a mission trip. It was eye opening for me—just what the doctor ordered. It was mind blowing to see people in far worse conditions expressing so much more happiness. They were overjoyed to interact with my team and me and to experience our songs and music. Of course, I felt bad for feeling down when I had so much to be thankful for. I realized that happiness and joy are relative to the person and situation.

We can change our outlook and perspective in a second. Have you ever been crying about something then received some good news that made those tears mysteriously dry up? Whatever caused the tears was still present, but the joy of the good news overshadowed that emotion. We only have one life and one opportunity to experience it. Let's not dwell on all the things that are not right, that cause pain, or that steal happiness. See the greatness in the simple things. Add to life more compassion, more inspiration, and more joy. Don't gloss over your experiences anymore. Embrace the good, the bad, and the ugly. Let's go beyond our limitations and reach for an outcome far greater than what we think is possible.

Doing Makes the Difference
Practice making the best of your life: Write down on a piece of paper the three worst things that happened to you today. In a column next to the list, write out one positive thing that correlates to each negative experience.

Check the Mirror
Are you beginning to see your true self emerge? Check the mirror. Does the woman staring back at you look more familiar than the one who was hiding behind the heavy

foundation, caked layers, and bright, distracting lipstick? Are you opening up to the idea of vulnerability for the sake of encouraging others? Are you ready to show the world your real beauty, your true self?

Finding our true selves involves (re)discovering our God-given passions. There are so many gifts, talents, and abilities deeply embedded inside of us. Some are innate qualities that are undeniable, while others are character-istics gleaned during childhood. No matter the origin, we often find ourselves running the race of life without ac-tivating these gifts. Many things can blot out these pas-sions from our lives. We've talked about basing our iden-tity on the expectations of others, focusing on highlighting something about ourselves that we want the world to see (something that may or may not be a part of our true nature), and healing from past hurts rather than masking our weaknesses.

Some of us have made the best out of passionless lives. We aimlessly get through life doing just that—getting through. We spend so much time trying to fit in with those we feel define our existence, yet we find little joy in their approval. Why go through the motions for your existence on Earth? Muster up enough courage to love deeply and live passionately because it has a positive effect on your emotional well-being. It enables you to gain experiences that will nourish your soul for years to come. In order to fuel this passion, however, you must know what your passion is. And you can't know that if you're hidden un-derneath the layers of the woman you've made yourself up to be.

Too often we wait for someone or something to intervene in our lives without realizing that we have this amazing power to provoke change in our own lives. We can make a decision to change our thoughts and actually bring about change in our circumstances. The responsibility to encourage belongs to each of us. It may sound strange, but we are accountable to ourselves for the purpose and direction of life being fulfilled. The most infectious and inspirational person to be around is the one who lives passionately for something outside of themselves, a greater cause.

Have you ever met someone with an innate fervor for something? I have, and it was inspiring. I met a woman while waiting in line to check out at the grocery store. Her name was Donna and her passion was helping children. I noticed she was purchasing a lot of food and, after a brief hello, it wasn't long before she expressed her passion. She'd already adopted seven children of crack-addicted parents. She decided her life was more meaningful and satisfying the more children she helped. I was fascinated by Donna's selfless love for children that were born into difficult situations. After hearing about her dedication to helping children, I immediately thought I needed to find passion outside of myself as well.

Doing Makes the Difference

For the next few weeks, plan to spend at least two hours a week doing what you are most passionate about. Dust off that manuscript you have been meaning to finish. Visit the women's shelter. Go back to school. Try to get pregnant again or catch up on your gardening. Do something!

A Bare-faced Community

Taking off the lipstick is a simple concept with a profound impact. Everything in our world today tells us to try to be anyone but ourselves. The media tells us to diet and look like a supermodel, our families tell us to be smarter and get a good job like our siblings, and even our friends at church tell us to only spend time with a certain type of person doing an activity they approve of. It's scary to go barefaced in a society where everyone wants to see you wearing a mask. Such a person will be met with some retribution, no doubt. It's possible that the people you have worked so hard to please will like you less if you don't conform to their image, but isn't the freedom worth it?

You want to stop hiding, but you don't want to do it alone. I completely understand. It's so important we take off the lipstick in community so we can all stop hiding together. We can start to remove the layers of past hurt, expectation, vanity, and pride. If we are all vulnerable together, then there is nothing for us to be afraid of. Community is intended to bind members and empower individuals through the tolerance of a collected group. We all have different passions, but we can all have the same appreciation for the gifts that each person brings to the community. God wants to cleanse each of us. He wants to give us the freedom to be the person He created us to be.

God wants to give you what your heart desires. He wants to connect you with people who love you. He wants everyone to feel his love through other people. If we start caring about, being honest with, and loving each other, then we can help each other. Some of us probably

HIDING BEHIND THE LIPSTICK

wouldn't have made the mistakes we did if we had had someone there to tell us the truth. That is why we let God take off the lipstick. He brings us out of our struggles to be a light to others in the midst of their own. If we are to be a community of genuine people, we must be willing to open up to one another and take part in a community of unashamed, bare-faced women who love the Lord and love each other. I am done hiding behind the lipstick. Aren't you?

Doing Makes the Difference

If you are the social butterfly, get a few of your friends together and tell them that you want to be honest and vulnerable with them. Ask if you can all be honest together. If it is helpful, begin by sharing the *Hiding Behind the Lipstick* DVD followed by a discussion. You can share something that you have never shared before. It doesn't have to be very deep. This will provide the opportunity for you to get to know the people around you and establish honesty among the group. Do it with someone so that your vulnerability can be matched and tested in community. No one should have to go through this process alone.

No matter the path you have taken, the cards you were dealt, the choices you have made, the pain you have endured, the money you've spent, or the time away from God, you can live free. You can and will rewrite this chapter of your life. There is so much ahead of you, for you to give, and for you to do. Please run this race with the joy and peace that has already been purchased for you. Embrace and accept the fact that there is more to living this life. Rest assured that who you are is absolutely perfect. Let those around you love the "you" that God created.

Time to Reflect

> Restore to me the joy of your salvation,
> and uphold me with a willing spirit...
> —Psalm 51:12 ESV

Name at least three lessons you've learned from this book that you will implement in your life:

1. _____

2. _____

3. _____

I will show the world that I am...

_____

_____

_____

_____

Write your own lipstick confession below:

_____

_____

_____

_____

_____

_____

_____

Dear Lord,

I am making a tough choice. I am turning from a way of living, thinking, and being that I have found comfortable for years of my life. I am starting a process of healing that will make me better. I am discovering just who I am. Please help me. I really don't know how. I am making peace with my painful past. I don't think I am ready. Help me. I must forgive others no matter how difficult and, most important, I must forgive myself. I have done things that I felt were unforgiveable. I am also letting go of the hurtful circumstances in my life. I won't use them as motivation to achieve more. I won't continue to use my life to prove others wrong. I will use them as a platform to love deeper. I am expecting that my life will have a richer meaning. I am expecting positive things to happen. Show me the purpose you have for me. Why did you create me? Ignite the flame within so I can influence change in this society. I want to make a difference. Help my friends to become open. I don't want to do this alone. Help my friends to live free too. Thank you for loving me through it all.

Amen

NOTES

1. "fake." Merriam-Webster.com. Merriam-Webster, 2013. Web.30 May 2013

2. "vulnerable." Merriam-Webster.com. Merriam-Webster, 2013. Web. 30 May 2013

3. "branding." Wikipedia: The Free Encyclopedia. Wikimedia Foundation, Inc., (26 May 2013). Web. (30 May 2013). http://en.wikipedia.org/wiki/Brand

4. "retail therapy." Wikipedia: The Free Encyclopedia. Wikimedia Foundation, Inc., (30 April 2013) Web. (30 May 2013). http://en.wikipedia.org/wiki/Retail_therapy

5. Guttmacher Institute, N.P. Web. 31 May 2013. <http://www.guttmacher.org/media/presskits/abortion-US/statsandfacts.html>.